Dear Superniki Purple

ANN McCELVEY WILLS

TYNDALE HOUSE PUBLISHERS
Wheaton, Illinois

Coverdale House Publishers Ltd., London, England

Library of Congress Catalog Card Number
79-123284 SBN 8423-0640-4 Copyright ©
1971 by Tyndale House Publishers, Wheaton,
Illinois 60187. All rights reserved. Third
printing, September 1971. Printed in the
United States of America.

With love and gratitude this book
is dedicated to my dearest friend
Evelyn McCelvey
who, incidentally, is also my mother.
Without her guidance and encouragement,
I might never have known of the thrill
and excitement of being a Christian.
My thanks and appreciation to her!

Dear Superniki Purple,

What does "Superniki Purple" mean and why should I waste my time reading this book?

You

Dear You,

Superniki Purple is what you and I are entitled to be. *Super* means "more than, extremely." *Niki* comes from the Greek word meaning "to be more than conqueror, to gain a surpassing victory." Put them together and the word means *"victorious plus!"* Jesus himself died on a cruel cross so that we might have an abundant life. "Take up your cross and follow Jesus" has been interpreted to mean "If you plan to follow Jesus, you'd better watch out! Life is going to be pretty rough; you'll be mistreated, defeated, and just plain miserable!" But let's look more closely at this cross.

When Jesus died, he paid the price for our salvation, our joy, and our victory. If we take up this cross, we are actually taking up what Jesus paid for. To assume that we, too, must pay the price means that we don't think Jesus Christ's life was enough to pay! He died that we might have life more abundantly — victorious in all situations. He died that we might become *superniki!*

The Scriptures are plentiful that promise a *superniki* life: "But despite all this, overwhelming victory is ours through Christ who loves us"; "No one who believes in Christ will ever be disappointed"; "Now glory be to God who by his mighty power at work within us is able to do far more than we would ever dare to ask or even dream of, infinitely beyond our highest prayers, desires, thoughts, or hopes"; "And we know that all that happens to us is working for our good if we love God, and if we are fitting into his plan."

Purple is the color of royalty. Anyone who is of royal blood doesn't have to waste time trying to impress the world with his worth. He doesn't have to have more than someone else, nor does he have to be more popular or pampered. The person who is aware that he is royal has real security, no inferiority complexes, no false sense of values. Instead, he has real happiness.

Abraham Lincoln said, "It is difficult to make a man miserable while he feels he is worthy of himself and claims kindred to the great God who made him."

You are of real royalty. Your Father is King of kings, Lord of lords, God. Therefore, you are entitled to act like royalty. Hold your head high for *you* are a child of *the King!*

We gave Mother our Volkswagen because we love her. It was during the winter and she took a long trip just a few days later. The trip turned out to be miserable. Her hands were numb, her feet were cold, and her entire body ached from the cold. When she told me about the trip, I asked her why she didn't use the heater. She admitted that she didn't even know how to turn it on.

Together we went out to the VW and I showed her the knob near the floor. It is so easy to turn, and once it is on, heat — lots of heat — comes pouring out. Mother had suffered — needlessly. Someone had to show her where the heater knob was. From then on, her driving was pleasant and comfortable.

That knob is typical of this book. We are entitled to a joyful, happy life. We ride in

"VWs," so to speak. Our heater has already been paid for by Jesus who died on Calvary.

Most people don't know how to turn on the heater of his love. They don't know how to turn their problems and cares over to him, and they don't know that they can trust him with the details of their lives.

In other words, this book is like one beggar telling another beggar where to find bread. I don't pretend to know all the answers but I know *the answer,* Jesus. Each knob printed in this book is printed in hopes that your life may become happier and that you will begin to *live* and not just *exist*.

Remember, Jesus loves *you!*

Dear Superniki Purple,

I am ashamed to admit this but I am terrified at the thought of being placed in a casket and buried under the ground. I believe in Heaven and yet I cannot get rid of my fear of being buried. Karl

Dear Karl,

Don't be ashamed of having the same fears that most people face. It is shocking that so many Christians are actually terrified of dying. I agree with you that the idea of being placed in an airtight box and placed in a six-foot hole and then having all that dirt piled on top of you is enough to send chills up and down your spine.

However, that's because you feel that *you* will be in that casket. When I cut my hair, I sweep it up and put it into the trash. The hair was a part of me but once it was cut from my head, it is no longer a part of me. Therefore, I don't care what the trashman does with my cut hair.

When I was a child, I had my tonsils removed. Losing them didn't do me a bit of harm. The tonsils were no longer necessary and so they were taken out. I don't know what the hospital did with my tonsils; I wanted no part of mine.

When I cut my fingernails, I throw the cut bits into the wastebasket. It doesn't upset me to destroy my cut hair, my unnecessary tonsils, nor my clipped fingernails.

With all my heart I believe that when this ticker of mine stops working, that is not the end of me — not of the Real Me. I will just be getting rid of the unnecessary parts.

When I cut my hair, I grow more hair. When my tonsils were removed, I got along without them. I believe that when I die, my body will no longer be necessary and so it will be discarded — buried — but *I* am not discarded.

I will not be in that grave any more than I am in the wastebasket with the fingernails, in the trash with the hair, or in the hospital disposal with the tonsils. The Real Me will go on to better things.

When this life on earth is over, I will leave this body that was needed to function here and I will take on a new form to function in my new life. When you come right down to it, graves contain nothing more than unnecessary parts.

The person whom we think of as being in a grave is not in that grave at all but has already gone on to something better — a life without pain or sorrow or troubles.

When I work out in the flowerbeds, I often get my shoes wet and muddy. When I start into the house, I leave my muddy shoes outside the door because I do not want to mess up the carpet.

I believe when the time comes for me to enter into that next life, I will leave my body outside in much the same manner that I leave my shoes outside when they are muddy.

Since I am now firmly convinced that I am not in that body that goes into the lonesome grave, I am no longer afraid of the grave itself. You need not be, either. For you will not be in the grave either!

Dear Superniki Purple,

Twenty years ago I was arrested for taking dope. Since getting out of prison, I have become a Christian and am active in my church. I live in horror that someone out of my past

*will pop up and spoil everything by telling my
friends what I did. What can I do?* Dean

Dear Dean,

You have no reason to hide nor to be uneasy when an old acquaintance shows up. You
said that you have become a Christian. That
means that you have confessed all your past
sins to God and he has forgiven you. If you
and God are on good terms, that's all that matters! Your Christian friends will have to be
Christlike, and since he has forgiven you, they
must forgive you, too.

Christians don't hold past mistakes against
anyone for they know that all of us have sinned
and God has forgiven those of us who have
asked for forgiveness. Some of us have very
bad things in our past while some of us never
did anything really bad. Yet we were all con-
demned sinners until God forgave us. If Christians had to be always perfect with nothing in
their past to be forgiven, sinners would have
no hope of becoming Christians. No matter
what your sins and mistakes have been —
whether large or small — Christ has forgiven
you if you have asked him to. He has made
you clean through and through. Your past is
of no importance. The only important thing is
your relationship with God. There may be
those who would be shocked at your past but

if they are really Christians they will accept you as a blood-washed Christian — as clean as anyone. If they don't, don't let their wrong attitudes of condemnation get to you. If God forgave you and all is well between you and God, it doesn't matter what they think. Don't hold grudges against those who will not forgive you. They are God's problem — not yours. It's up to God to straighten out their wrong attitudes and un-Christlike actions. Just love them and continue to love the Lord and forget your past.

The most important thing for you to do is to forgive yourself. You do not have to be ashamed of your past. If you confessed your sins, God forgave you. If he forgave you, you must forgive yourself. We pray, "Forgive us . . . as we forgive." Since you still feel the guilt and shame, you have not actually forgiven yourself and you are telling God not to forgive you. It is just as important that you forgive your mistakes as it is for you to ask God to forgive them. You can't be completely happy until you do.

We often feel that we should carry guilt around as punishment for our mistakes. We think we are "above" making some of our dumb mistakes. As we look back on life, we see many opportunities that were overlooked. We see mistakes in raising our children. We

remember unkind deeds. We feel the shame
of a hasty word that was misunderstood, and
we see all the mistakes we have made. We
know that we have confessed our sins but
somehow we cannot bring ourselves to forgive
us.

Instead of being miserable, tell the Lord
that you regret all the mistakes you have made.
Ask his forgiveness now — no matter how long
ago something happened. Then accept his forgiveness and at the same time forgive yourself.
When God forgives you, he forgets. You, too,
must forget. That doesn't mean that you won't
remember the deed or action but it does mean
that you will remember without any feeling of
shame or guilt.

An outstanding minister said that mistakes
are just stepping-stones. Instead of feeling
guilty for the rest of your life, Dean, accept the
fact that you are not perfect, but God loves
you anyway. Then use the mistakes to lead
you into a deeper walk with God. Don't hold
unforgiving feelings for your imperfections but
forgive yourself even as God for Christ's sake
has forgiven you!

Dear Superniki Purple,
Do you believe that God will speak to us through nature? Fred

Dear Fred,

I would not dare limit the manner in which God will speak to us. He speaks in so many different ways. We usually just don't recognize his voice. I definitely believe he speaks through nature because he has spoken to me through wild flowers.

When it became necessary for us to move, we prayed for guidance concerning the house we would buy and the location. When we found the house that "felt" right, we bought it. However, after a few months, doubts and fears began to creep into my heart. I discovered that the payments were higher than I had realized and that it was a very long drive to work. Many other factors became exaggerated in my mind until I was feeling very depressed. It seemed that we had really goofed.

As I dressed for work one morning, all of the problems concerning the house hit me at once. I felt so sure that we had made a mistake and I had the frustrating feeling that it was too late to do anything about it. I was rather sick inside as I drove out of the driveway on my way to work.

The street we live on has houses on only one side. Across the street there is nothing but woods. Suddenly my eyes caught a most unusual sight directly in front of the house. Waving gently in the breeze were the most beautiful tall, purple wild flowers. I paused and admired them and drove on toward work. As I drove down the street, I searched for other purple flowers but none were in sight. This bugged me all day. To satisfy my curiosity, that afternoon I drove slowly down the street searching for some other purple flowers. There were none anywhere except directly in front of our house. It was as though Someone had planted them there just for me.

I was so thrilled! Why? Well, I have a "thing" about purple. If it were left up to me, everything we own would be purple — and almost everything is already. All my friends know that I am a fanatic about purple. "All my friends" includes the Lord. He knew that I would notice those lovely purple flowers and that I would take it as a message straight from him that we are exactly where he wants us to be. Since we had prayed for guidance, he had given it to us. There was no room for doubts or fears. If God chose this very spot for us, then he would be with us. If he is with us, there is nothing to fear or worry about.

Fred, it's exciting to recognize God. He tries to get through to us in many different ways. Never doubt his ability to speak in any manner he chooses. You can always tell if it is the Lord because he will never contradict the Bible nor embarrass anyone. God is a good God and he loves you more than you can possibly imagine.

Dear Superniki Purple,

My boss just chewed me out and I'm very hurt. I just want to complain to someone and you were elected. Lisa Lou

Dear Lisa Lou,

Most of us get unhappy about situations now and then. I know that I have often become so mad and complained so much that I was ashamed of myself.

One day in particular I was furious! I was so mad that I was fuming inside. As I drove home from work, I began to rehash the unpleasant situation. The more I thought about it, the madder I became. I began to complain to the Lord telling him that I wasn't being treated fairly, etc. I was all set to complain in detail to Don when I got home. It just wasn't fair!

However, I hadn't driven very far when I remembered that I had asked God to control my life on that very same road — that very same day. Several hours earlier I had told God that I wanted him to be the Boss of my life. Now it seemed that I was saying that I didn't like the way he ran things. I was complaining, which in reality meant, "Lord, I know I gave my life to you this morning but you made such a mess out of it that I withdraw my dedication. I don't like the way you allowed me to be mistreated. You weren't a very good Boss, so from now on, I'll be the boss. I guess you aren't as smart as I thought you were."

Shocking? Honestly now, wasn't that what I was saying with my complaining — except that I put it in "nicer" words — or was I? If I really meant business when I asked God to be the Boss of my life, didn't that mean that no matter what he chose for me, no matter what situation came up, I would cheerfully acknowledge him? Who am I to question God? Anytime I complain, I am actually saying that God isn't capable of handling my life. When the situation becomes unpleasant, does that mean that God has gone to sleep and forgot all about little ole me? When I am mistreated, where is God? Guess God isn't capable of handling lives today?

Oooooo no! When I realized what I was doing, I was so ashamed. I know that God is more than capable of handling my life. If I sincerely asked him to be the Boss, then I believe that he actually controls every detail of my life — everything that happens and every word that is or is not spoken. Nothing can involve me unless God okays it — that is, *if* he's the Boss.

There seems to be just one tiny catch — "Giving thanks always for *all* things." As long as I was complaining, I certainly was not giving thanks. I complained because I didn't realize who the Boss was. As long as I thought the people who were giving me a rough time were doing so all on their own, then I was unhappy and complaining. But once I realized that God is the Boss and whatever he allows is for my good, then I could honestly give thanks to him for the temporarily unpleasant situation and seemingly raw deal. (All things work together for good . . .)

The strange and wonderful thing about giving thanks is that the thanks removes all hurt and madness. You can't thank God for allowing things to happen and at the same time have resentment or complain. There is absolutely no room for any complaining of any kind when God is the Boss!

I don't mean that I never complain. Sometimes I forget that God is the Boss over every detail — but only briefly. Now that I know that I can trust God with the details of my life, there is no point in getting upset and complaining. Since I can trust God, what can I possibly complain about? If I don't like the way things are going, I can ask God to do something about it but I can't tell him how nor complain if he doesn't do things exactly as I think best. I have to leave all decisions up to him — *if* he's the Boss.

When you discover that God loves you very much and is interested in your life, you'll be so busy thanking him for his love and concern that you won't have time nor desire to complain.

Dear Superniki Purple,

There are so many disappointments in life. I don't get over them easily. Is there any secret that I don't know about? I hate disappointments. Bess

Dear Bess,

Someone said that the word "disappointments" should be changed into "his appointments." Life is filled with disappointments because we try to plan our lives and things don't always work out exactly as we plan.

I remember my first great disappointment. It happened when I was a senior in Crockett High School. There were to be three plays put on by the school for the city. The judges would choose one play to go to County Meet. There one play would be selected to go to state, and so on. I read all three plays and the leading part in one play seemed to be made just for me. I was perfect for the part . . . or so I thought. I wanted that part more than I had ever wanted anything before. The tryouts came and all of my friends assured me

that the part would be mine. I was a "ham"
anyway and this was a real tear-jerker part.
I had to have it! But shock of shocks, I
didn't get the part. I went home feeling rejected, unhappy, upset, and everything else
bad. As usual, I bent Mother's ear with my
complaints. I was almost sick with disappointment.

Mother listened sympathetically for a few
minutes and then told me that it was time that
I "turned loose." I had no idea what she
meant but I was so unhappy that I was willing to try anything. She told me to clench
both of my fists as tightly as I could. Then I
was to imagine that my disappointment, anger,
ego, resentment, wrong attitudes, *and* that part
in the play were all in my fists. For a brief moment I was just to clench my fist, and know
that I had problems.

Then I was to say a little prayer: "Father,
in my fists are all my wrong attitudes, my hurt,
my problems. I can't change the way I feel
about this situation but you can. Please help
me." With that I was to imagine the contents
of my fist falling — not into thin air — but
into the mighty, capable hands of God. She
told me to hold my hands open until I could
actually feel a lightness of heart. Then she
told me to turn my open hands and pray,
"Father, here is my empty heart and life.

Please fill me with your love and your wisdom and your attitudes. Thank you for changing me."

With all honesty and sincerity I tried this and was amazed. I can't explain exactly how it happened, but I know that I was a different person. The resentment was really gone. The hurt to my pride was gone. I felt good again.

A few days passed and the principal was notified that the schedule for the County Meet had been changed. An important scholastic event coincided with the play. The girl who had won the part had to choose between an important competition for the school and being in the play. She gave up the play without thinking twice. It wasn't important to her anyway.

Needless to say, I was given the part in the play. Our play won in the city and in the county and went on to state, where we lost. I was selected best actress in the city and county and honorable mention in state. I firmly believe that God allowed me to win not because I was really good but because he was proving his love for me. As long as I "turn loose" my own ideas and am willing to take what God dishes out, then I will be so much better off — always — in every phase of life.

The process of "turning loose" was not a

once-in-a-lifetime thing. It has become a part of my everyday living. There are disappointments every day. But when we put our lives and our trust in God, the Bible promises, "He will never disappoint you." We can count on him; he knows what is best for us!

Dear Superniki Purple,

My precious eight-year-old daughter died. I visit her grave often and always carry flowers. I am spending much of my time at her grave. I worry about her all the time. What is she doing now? Is she all right? Please help me. I can't sleep for worrying about her. Marilyn

Dear Marilyn,

There were two caterpillars crawling along in the cabbage patch. One said to the other, "Charlie, one of these days I'm not going to be a lowly worm scooting along in the dirt eating dirty, tough cabbages. One of these days I'm going to be beautiful and I'm going to fly gracefully through the air and sip honey from the delicate flowers."

To this Charlie replied, "Fred, you've been hitting the bottle again. You must be off your rocker! You're out of your tree, man. What's gotten into you!"

But by and by, Fred died. There was a nice "funeral" and all of his friends said that that was the end of nutty ole Fred. But we know better. In time his "grave" did burst open and out came a delicate and beautiful little butterfly. And Fred did fly through the air and sip nectar from the flowers.

Now if God loves that caterpillar enough to make his next life that much better than his first one, how much more does he love your daughter! Your daughter is very precious to God — even more than she is to you. God loves her so much that he sent Jesus to die that she might have eternal life. God loves your daughter, Marilyn. Whatever the next life is, it will be exciting and good. If we could talk with people who have already died, I am sure that they would tell us of the thrill of being with Jesus. They would tell us of such exciting things that we would all wish to die. I believe God didn't let us know all there is to know about the next life because we would be more interested in dying than in living.

While your dear little girl was with you, you were careful to see that she received the very best that you could give her. You were always looking for ways to make her life better and happier, weren't you? How you should rejoice to realize that no matter how much you could do for her while she was in your care, the heavenly Father is now caring for her in wonderful ways you can't even imagine. The apostle Paul mentioned in one of his letters how much he was looking forward to leaving this life and going to be with Christ, which he said would be "far better." Commit your daughter to God's care and know for a fact that it is "far better" for her now that she is with him.

Of course you will miss your child, but you will receive peace from knowing that she is happy with the Father. If you are God's child by faith in Jesus, you will someday join your daughter and discover for yourself the wonders of the next life.

Dear Superniki Purple,
   My life is such a mess. I will never amount to anything. The harder I try, the bigger mess I make. I'm a flop. Agnes

Dear Agnes,

   You are God's flop and he loves you. However, I doubt seriously that you really are a flop. You just see yourself as you are this very minute. You don't realize what God is making out of you.

   I bought an ugly black filing cabinet with the intention of painting it and turning it into something nice. I had high hopes. With a red-gold paint kit, I set out to make it into a work of art. The first coat of paint was reddish orange. After several back-breaking hours of hard work, I was utterly disgusted. The ugly black was bleeding through the new paint and the result was pitiful. Even my neighbors felt sorry for me for wasting my time on the hopeless piece of junk.

   So I just gave up for a few days. It bugged me, though, and so I decided to finish it just to get it out of the way. The second coat was a clear varnish with small gold flakes. I tested it on something else and couldn't tell any difference. But as I sat applying the paint, my eyes couldn't believe what I was seeing! That horrid old piece of junk was turning into something lovely. The gold flake paint was just enough to change the dull sick color into a sparkling, happy combination. What a difference it made! Eagerly I finished it still not believing the results I was seeing. Looking at the finished product, you would never guess that it was once tagged a hopeless piece of junk. The gold shine over the dull orange turned out to be just what I wanted — a masterpiece.

I suppose we all have looked at our lives and thought, "What a hopeless piece of junk!" We try to amount to something but the more we try, the more disgusted we become. We look for immediate results and can't see any. We can only see *right now*. There's no way for us to know how God is using us nor do we know how he is preparing us for something better.

But this is looking at the filing cabinet with the first coat of paint on it. If we stop right there, life isn't worth very much and we don't have much to look forward to. We all get disgusted with the unfair things that happen in the world. But we cannot see the finished products in our lives nor in the lives of others. In the case of the filing cabinet, if I had known how beautiful it was going to become, I would not have become so discouraged. I would have finished it eagerly. But I did not know because I cannot see into the future. But God knows what we will be like when he is finished with us. Everything that happens to us is part of his plan.

Agnes, God loves you very much and his will for your life is what you would choose for yourself if you knew what he had planned. You don't have to become discouraged nor disgusted. When you give your life to God, the results are up to him. He is going to spend all of your life making you into his masterpiece!

Dear Superniki Purple,

My marriage is certainly nothing to brag about. We're married and that's about all I can say for us. We aren't really unhappy but we aren't happy, either. Are we just getting old and used to each other? Rella

Dear Rella,

Too many people feel as you do. The trend nowadays is to look for the failures instead of the good points. Even entertainers dwell on ridicule and failures rather than the pleasant things. It's the trend to be unhappy and to criticize.

I was falling into that rut during the first years of our marriage. After the honeymoon, there was the Army and with the Army came the lack of money and moving away from home. There were problems, sure, and with the problems came the complaining. I found myself a thousand miles from home and friends, unhappy with my job and with life in general. In that state of mind, it was impossible to be a good wife.

One cold, snowy day the Sarge called to tell me that Don was being shipped out to the Middle East. The rumors had been going around for a long time. Sarge was a good friend of ours and wanted me to know that this wasn't a practice alert but that Don wouldn't be back. They were in a Strike

Group which meant that he could be gone in twenty-four hours. Sarge wanted me to take Don to the base to save the red tape of getting the car back and so that I could tell him "good-bye" properly. He went on to say that they would probably be overseas a year. It seemed that he went on and on but I heard little else. My heart was broken! My tears flowed as though a dam had broken. I was crushed!

It had hit me. Don was leaving and I might never see him again. I realized just how much I loved him and how much I didn't want him to leave. The fact that we were in a snowy city far from home with little money and few acquaintances was of little importance. The only thing that mattered was that Don was leaving!

I couldn't stand the thought of losing him and I just didn't know what to do. So I cried and cried. Presently Don came in. When he saw the pitiful look on my face, he took the tear-soaked phone. He talked just a few minutes and then laughingly said, "Sure thing, Sarge," and hung up. I was stunned. How could he laugh! Then Don told me the story and soon my tears turned to anger. There was no strike alert — practice nor real! Sarge was just playing a joke on me. There was nothing to the rumor of their going to the

Middle East. He was just teasing.

What a rotten joke! I was furious! But the fury was short-lived. Suddenly I saw myself and our marriage in a different perspective. I wasn't happy with my former attitudes nor the complaining part I had played as a wife.

Don could have gone off to war and never returned. There is no guarantee on life. I thought, "Anytime he goes to work could be the last time I will ever see him. He could easily be killed in a car wreck. Many people die in their sleep. There is absolutely no guarantee on anyone's life." And so I started a new way of thinking and acting.

My thoughts were these: "If my husband should die today, what would I wish I had told him? While there is still time, I'm going to tell him. If he should die today, how would I wish I had acted at home? We should enjoy each day and we should live each day as though it were the last. Who knows, it could be!"

Rella, if you will treat your husband with the same love and kindness that you would if you knew that this would be your last day together, I believe you will find a new dimension in marriage. I know that your home will be happier and you will find a new joy and delight in being married.

Believe me, it's worth a try!

Dear Superniki Purple,

God seems to ignore my prayers. I'm a Christian and yet it seems that I pray in vain. I never see results. Why? Jean

Dear Jean,

God wants you to love and trust him even though you don't see immediate results. He doesn't always answer as we expect him to answer.

I was once involved in a crisis at work. A deadline was dangerously near and a paper valued at $3,000 was misplaced. I frantically searched for the missing paper, but it was nowhere to be found. I had to have the information on it before we could collect the money. By the weekend, I had worried myself sick. Mother knew of the importance of the paper and together we prayed. We believed that God would help me find the paper. We had prayed for similar things before and God had always come to the rescue.

Monday I went to work feeling confident that the paper would be found. There was only one man who could reconstruct a vital part of the information and he had just left for a two weeks' vacation. He wouldn't be back until after the deadline. I couldn't wait. All too soon, everyone knew what a dum-dum I was. The big boss at the other plant put several men on the job of reconstructing all the information. They had to go to a lot of extra work and I was extremely embarrassed — and rather disappointed that God didn't let the paper turn up.

The second paper was not complete when it was given to me. I checked it out and gave it to our cost accounting department for the final figures. Presently the head of the department came over questioning what I had done. It seemed that my information didn't agree with the original paper. After checking very thoroughly, we discovered that the first paper had been incorrect. A very important part had been omitted. If the original paper had been found, we would have cheated ourselves out of $2,800. If God had answered my prayer the way I asked him to, the company would have been out $2,800, although I would have been saved some embarrassment. Since God ignored my dictation and answered for the best, my faith grew and the company was better off. I don't have to dictate to God how he should run my job nor my life. I can just trust him!

The best was yet to come. About two months later the boss handed me a piece of paper and said, "I don't know what this is but it seems to belong to you." I couldn't believe my eyes. There was the missing paper! It never reached my desk because it had been stuck in a bottom drawer.

Jean, God hears your prayers and he is answering — but in his own way and in his own timing. You can trust him. You aren't praying in vain. God loves you so much that he wants to teach you to trust him.

Dear Superniki Purple,

What color will I be in Heaven? I'm really concerned about my appearance there. Will there be any racial problems there? Joan

Dear Joan,

Jesus is concerned with your soul. What color is your soul? To determine what color and shape you will be, you will have to determine the appearance of your soul. For it is your soul which will go on to the next life. Your physical body will be discarded in the grave just as all unnecessary parts are discarded while you yet live. The Real You consists of your soul.

Joan, don't worry about what you will look like in Heaven. Whatever God chooses for you there will be exciting and wonderful. You will not have to compete with anyone for physical acceptance. You will not have to be more beautiful nor of any particular nationality. All of those barriers will be left in the grave with the unnecessary body.

Dear Superniki Purple,
My pastor does several little things that annoy me. I have complained and hinted but it

*hasn't done any good. How can I get through
to him?* Mary

Dear Mary,

It seems to me that you have been complaining to the wrong person! If you go into
the grocery store and see something that you
dislike, it would be useless to complain to the
carry-out boy. You can bellyache to the
checker but all you will accomplish is ill will
and an unpleasant atmosphere. If you have
a complaint, you must go to the store manager
for results. He is responsible for the policies
of the store.

The same principle applies to your pastor
and to every other Christian. When he became a Christian, he gave himself to God.
That makes him God's responsibility! If you
dislike something he does, tell God! Don't
make the situation worse by talking about
him among your friends or by criticizing him.
Go straight to the Boss. God will listen to
your complaints. Then he'll either change the
pastor — or your attitude.

The old Indian saying about not judging a
man until you have walked a day in his moc-
casins is good advice for all of us. Mary, instead of looking for faults, why not dwell on
your pastor's good qualities? The Bible says,
"Whatsoever things are good — think on
these!"

Dear Superniki Purple,

I would love to tell the people who come into my place of business about the love of God. There is never any opportunity. How can I possibly help any of them? Allene

Dear Allene,

Early one morning a man used my telephone before I got to work. As soon as I reached my desk, the phone rang and the moment I answered, I knew that someone had used my phone recently. The aroma of after shave lotion was unmistakable! When I completed my call, I asked the lady who sits next to me who had used my phone. She was startled by my question. When I explained that the aroma was still there, she chuckled and said that a certain man had hung up just before I walked in.

Allene, so it is when you are filled to overflowing with the love of God. When you have "been with Jesus," you have an aroma much sweeter and more effective than after shave lotion. You can be so filled with God that his spirit and love will overflow from you to everyone you meet. His love will go over the phone to those with whom you speak. They may not be aware of it for it is very subtle and many do not recognize the love of God. Even after they leave you, the fragrance will linger.

The busy world needs the fragrance of his love. You may not say a word. But God's love will flow from your spirit to those you contact. God's presence in you will lift low spirits, will put a sparkle in a dull day, and will give love to the lonely and hope to the hopeless. The fragrance of God's love is the best perfume in all the world — and it's yours — free. All you have to do is be so filled with God's love that it will freely overflow to all around you.

Dear Superniki Purple,

I have a chance for some on-the-job train-ing that could lead to quite a promotion. The only drawback is that I would have to go out of the state for several months, leaving my family behind. Do you think I should go? Joe

Dear Joe,

I cannot tell you what to do — but I can tell you what I would do if I were in your shoes.

First of all, the Texas law recognizes that your wife shares half of all you possess. If the law thinks this much of your wife, you as a Christian should think at least this much — and more. Therefore, your first considera-tion should be your wife's feelings. Talk with her and go over the pros and cons of this op-portunity. After you have talked together, pray together. Make it clear to God as well as to yourselves that you want whatever he chooses for you. Then expect guidance from him. "As your faith, so be it unto you."

I believe that guidance will come first of all in peace of mind. If you both feel really good about your going, then believe that God has given you the okay to go. But if there is hesitation or dread, recognize that God is tell-ing you that this is not the great opportunity that you think it is. Now, if God okays your move, he will also open the doors so that you will be able to go. If you find obstacles in your way, realize that God put them there so that you would know that he does not want you to go. When he leads, he always makes a way.

If everything works out and you have the opportunity and you and your wife both feel good about your going, thank the Lord for his guidance and go in peace. Go knowing that the same God who loves you will be with your family in your absence.

Dear Superniki Purple,

I know the Bible says that man is to be the head of the house — the boss. However, I know that I am smarter than my husband. Isn't that Scripture outdated? Barbara

Dear Barbara,

I, too, faced this dilemma recently. I allowed my husband to be the "boss" over a few areas but then I began to wonder if there wasn't a limit. When Don decided that it was time for a new car, I decided that the limit had been reached. I was violently opposed to buying a new car. I have never liked new cars and the thought of those high car payments turned me against them even more. Despite all the logic Don gave me, I would not budge. I knew that our car could not last forever and that it was using oil, needed tires and a paint job, and that the valves were burnt and the transmission was not working properly. But all of this made no difference. The car still ran and I did not want a new one and that was that!

Then one morning Don had to go to work very early. After he left, I couldn't go back to sleep. As I lay awake listening to the rain, I suddenly became aware of some strange noises. I was certain that someone was trying to break into our house. A terrible fear gripped me. When I'm afraid, there's only one thing to do and that is to pray. I did not stir but lay motionless in bed praying. As I prayed, I became aware that my God is greater than anyone who tries to break into my house. As I began to acknowledge this fact, all of my fear left.

But then I realized that I did not have the same faith when it came to my husband. God is greater than Don and can therefore control him. The Bible says that "he will give you the desire of your heart." I believe that means that God will plant the desire in the heart and then bring it to pass. (Bear in mind that God will never allow you to want anything contrary to the Bible. If you want something that doesn't go along with the Bible, then God did not plant that desire in your heart.) Somehow I had never connected that Scripture with Don's desire for a new car.

I don't have to worry about the car payments for if God allows Don to want a new car, then God will help us to manage our money to pay for that car. A marvelous thing about paying tithes is that it is the best investment ever. By paying tithes, we are acknowledging that God is a partner in our finances as well as every other phase of our lives. This means that God is able to supply the wisdom for managing our money.

All my anxiety about a new car has gone. But even better, I now know that God ordained the man to be the head of the house and that is the way it must be. When the man is aware that he's the head, he will not be domineering because he will not have to prove that he's the boss. When he runs things, he will be more considerate and lovable. I have learned that I can trust God to lead Don. If God wanted Don to be head of the house, who am I to tell God and Don when we need a new car?

Dear Superniki Purple,

My neighbor is such a snob that it makes me sick. She thinks she's so "high and mighty" that I'd like to knock her off her high horse. She is the biggest snob in town. How can I cut her down to size? Connie

Dear Connie,

Once I worked for a large company involved in rigid government contracts. Every department was under a great deal of pressure. At lunch a group of us would eat together and laugh and cut up, trying to release some of the tensions that had built up during the morning. There was a fellow named Charlie who was known as a "wet blanket — a snob." When Charlie joined us, the laughter ceased. We all felt that he didn't like nor approve of us. His remarks were never harsh enough to be ugly and yet never kind enough to be friendly. So we tagged him as a First Class Snob.

One Monday Charlie was not at work. It wasn't until then that we learned that he had been postponing a serious heart operation. His good friend had died during the same operation only a month before. That death had frightened Charlie immensely. But none of us dreamed that Charlie was even considering such an operation. Why, Charlie was the picture of health — a husky, handsome, healthy-looking young man in his early twenties. None of us could have guessed his fears — especially since we were so busy tagging him as a snob.

On Tuesday we learned — too late — that Charlie was not a snob. Charlie died in surgery.

When people growl or say unkind things to us for no apparent reason, we are quick to jump to the conclusion that they don't like us. So often we, in our self-centeredness, take another's actions as a personal insult. The person who appears to be a snob may be bottling up a problem, such as the fear of death. If we knew that someone was going to die, we would not be annoyed if he were abrupt. If we knew that the person who is unkind had a bad ulcer, we would overlook his rudeness.

Connie, instead of being annoyed with your neighbor, treat her with the same kindness and forgiveness that you would if you knew that she was dying. It's worth a try. As long as you are annoyed, you will never become "Superniki." If someday you find out what was troubling your neighbor, you will be very glad that you acted as a Christian should.

Dear Superniki Purple,
  I'm getting old and I hate being old. Make-up doesn't hide my years. How can I stay young? Marta

Dear Marta,

Today we place a false emphasis on being young and beautiful. This is so unimportant. Is there anyone you really love *just* because she is young and beautiful? We normally love someone because of his personality and the fact that he loves us. We normally enjoy being with someone because he approves of us and likes us. It's nice to have a beautiful appearance but it is not the ultimate. My most cherished friends could not win any beauty contests and yet I would not trade them for all the beautiful people in the whole world.

This reminds me of two gifts I received once. One gift was wrapped only in brown paper and came in a plain box. The other was exquisitely wrapped with a large expensive ornament. The beautifully wrapped package contained a gift of little importance while the plainly wrapped package contained a gift that I value greatly because of its worth and the fact that it was given and received in love.

The same applies to us — to you and to me. When we were very young, God in his kindness wrapped us in the beauty of youth. But we do not have to fear losing that beauty because as we grow older, the inside package becomes more valuable and the outer wrappings lose significance.

The fact that you may have lost your girlish figure, you may have a few wrinkles, you may have some gray hair, is of little importance. "Beauty is in the eyes of the beholder," and if you are not beautiful on the inside, all the makeup in the world will not make you beautiful.

One of the best "cosmetics" that I know of is the prayer of St. Francis:

"Lord, make me an instrument of thy peace. Where there is hatred, let me sow love; where there is injury, pardon; where there is doubt, faith; where there is despair, hope; where there is darkness, light; where there is sadness, joy."

If this can be accomplished through us, Marta, we will become a beautiful gift of real and lasting importance no matter what our age nor how we are "wrapped up."

Dear Superniki Purple,

No one really cares about me. I feel so rejected and unloved. Why doesn't anyone care? Agnes

Dear Agnes,

Someone cares about you — and cares very much. That Someone is Jesus! He died on the cross that you might enjoy living and might have the hope of eternal life. Jesus loves you and cares about the details of your life. He cares about *you*.

The last time President Kennedy was in Houston, we accidentally saw him. We were on our way home when we noticed a large crowd gathering at an intersection in front of us. When we reached the crowd, a policeman told us to just park in the middle of the street because we could not pass until the President had passed. We jumped out of the car into a scene of enthusiasm and excitement. It only took a moment for us to fall into the mood of the atmosphere. Soon the thrill had enveloped us and we, too, stood eagerly waiting to see the President of the United States.

As the time drew near, several policemen zoomed by with their sirens screaming, which only built up the anticipation. Then the loud cheers reached our ears and we knew that he was coming! And then, there in a long black limousine was the President of the United States! Amidst the thrill and the loud cheers, there was an exciting feeling of awe. I had butterflies in my tummy from the thrill of seeing someone really important.

In a very brief moment it was all over. But we were left with an afterglow of thrill and reverence for we had seen the President.

Oh, how much more exciting it is when the God of the universe passes by! The President was much too busy to stop and listen to me and my problems. If he had spoken to me, I would have been overwhelmed. Why, he did not even know that I existed. And if he had known, he could not have stopped to talk with me. But even if he had stopped, he could not have solved my problems. He could not have given me lasting peace, joy, and happiness. He could not have been with me at a moment's notice.

But God knows that I exist. He knows that you exist. He is never too busy to listen to you and to me. He can solve *all* of our problems and he will, because he loves us (that is, if we will let him). We do not have to wait until a rare occasion when he is in town. He is always right here, ready to solve our problems. He is a very present help — always.

Agnes, you have no right to be lonely and unhappy. The God of the universe loves you and he cares about you! Get acquainted with him and your lonely days will be over forever.

Dear Superniki Purple,
Some people seem to take troubles so well. Not me; I go to pieces and become bitter and miserable. What's the difference? Mildred

Dear Mildred,
When we lived in Colorado, there was an early thirty-two-inch snow. Everyone was caught off guard — even the trees. Our large yard was a disaster — limbs were everywhere. Across the street was the most beautiful yard I have ever seen. The spruce trees had just enough snow on them to make them look like those on a Christmas card. It was breathtaking

to look at the scenery . . . I have never seen anything quite so picturesque.

In our yard there were tall, strong trees with long branches far from each other. When the snow fell, it piled up on the leaves and the weight became too much for one branch alone and so the branch fell. Across the street, the spruce had tiny branches close to each other and slanting downward in humility. The same snow fell on them. When it piled up, instead of breaking the branches, the snow slid right off leaving just enough to make the trees beautiful.

We can be like that. If we are independent and feel that we know it all and need no one, not even God, we are like the branch that goes out all alone. When trouble comes, we can't hold up alone and so we crack up. Or we can be like the humble spruce — we can stay close to each other and close to the Tree Trunk, God. Then when troubles come, we don't have to bear the load alone but we have other Christians to help hold us up and we have God who is the only real answer for troubles of any kind.

If we have something that we should get rid of, we'd better do so immediately because we don't want to be caught off guard and unprepared. If we are depending on money instead of God, if we resent someone, if we have not forgiven everyone, or if we haven't completely turned our lives over to God, we are unprepared.

Remember, Mildred, the same thing, the snow, that destroyed one tree only made the other one more beautiful!

Dear Superniki Purple,

Is everything "God's will"? It seems that if God didn't want something to happen, he wouldn't allow it, but with all the violence, murders, wars, riots, etc., I wonder. John

Dear John,

God certainly has *not* willed all the violence in the world. And even Christians do not always live in God's will. You see, John, God wanted a people who would love and obey him because they wanted to and not because they had to. So when he created us, he gave us a free will. We are free to love, dislike, or make decisions. Our mental attitude towards others and situations is entirely up to us. We have the choice of loving God and asking him to direct our lives or we can ignore him and take a chance on making a miserable mess of our lives — and even ending up violently.

God's decision to give us a free will reminds me of the love of a baby. I remember when my nephew Larry was a baby. Larry loved everyone. It didn't matter who you were or what you had done, Larry loved you and had a way of showing it. It was no compliment to you that Larry loved you — he loved everyone. But when Larry grew up and his mind developed, he didn't love just anybody. He chose his friends carefully. He had a mind of his own. He chose those he wanted to associate with and those he wanted to love. Therefore, when he chose to include me in the group of loved ones, I was flattered. The satisfaction of being loved by him is much greater now that he has a mind of his own.

I think God must have felt something like that when he decided to give us the right to choose for ourselves. When we choose God, it proves that we are intelligent and that we are living up to his expectation for the human race.

Even young people can be in God's will. It is so simple. Add this to your prayers, John: "Jesus, I don't know very much about your will in my life. But I love you and want you to guide me in all that I do. I want to be more like you want me to be. Please help me. Thank you."

The people causing violence are merely looking for an answer to the longing deep within. The only answer is Jesus. When they discover him and his great love for them, they will no longer want to kill and riot. God isn't pleased with the crime in the world today, John. But he is pleased when people like you make the right choice and ask him to control your life.

Dear Superniki Purple,

My husband and I argue constantly about money. He doesn't understand how expensive everything is and he thinks I'm extravagant. I'm ready to crown him. He is especially critical of the grocery bill. How can I get through to him that everything costs more now? Dot

Dear Dot,

Most housewives handle the money in the family and most of them try to protect their husbands from the bother of little details. The husband is too busy or too tired to fool with buying groceries and paying the light bill. The well-meaning wife doesn't bother him with the cost of everything. Especially at the end of the year when the husband sees how much money he has made, he starts asking questions like "Where did all the money go?" and "How could you spend so much?" This can and will upset most wives. To say that the groceries were high and that the bills come around regularly just isn't enough. Tension and misunderstanding builds up and a marriage can be seriously damaged.

It isn't wise for one person to handle all money matters without the other being periodically informed. One couple solved this problem by shopping together once a month. The husband would get an idea of what groceries were costing his family. He quit complaining about the grocery bill when he saw the actual cost of groceries. Then he paid all the bills once during the summer and once during the winter. They made a practice of never complaining about money. Paying the bills was not a bitter, unpleasant time but an accepted fact. During the year the wife would pleasantly mention when they needed to purchase anything out of the ordinary. A good deal of tension disappeared and their marriage became better than before.

You must remember that marriage is a partnership and you both must share. Overprotection is not a kindness. Your husband has the right to know where the money goes. You aren't alone, you know. As you put your trust in God, he will help you with the financial problems and he will give you wisdom in your spending. You can't complain and seek his guidance at the same time. "Giving thanks always for all things" must be your motto.

Dear Superniki Purple,

You talk as though life is a "bed of roses." Well, you're wrong. The people I work with are giving me fits. I just can't buy all this stuff about Superniki. Dale

Dear Dale,

I am not suggesting that life is a bed of roses — far from it. But I do believe that our lives should be like "one rose." Most people love roses. I know I do. When I see a rose, my first reaction is, "Oh, isn't that pretty." But at the same time, my intelligence knows that the rose has thorns and that thorns are undesirable. A thorn in my thumb is a most unpleasant feeling — it hurts!

Now, life is like that rose. There are thorns in everyday life — you can count on that. There are people who will rub us the wrong way and there are problems of every kind. But if God is in control of our lives, his love will overshadow those thorns.

One common thorn is people who get under our skin. I suppose all of us have had someone who bugged us. We may try to avoid that person but when we give our lives to God, he will not let us avoid people we do not like. He wants us to live a *Superniki* life — and that doesn't mean avoiding unpleasant people. Therefore, God in his lovingkindness will put us into direct contact with that person we can not stand.

Years ago, in my office there was a girl whom I avoided like the plague. She was catty and downright ugly. Much to my disgust, she was transferred into my department and seated right in front of me. I just got sick. Of all the hundreds of employees, she was the only one that I really couldn't stomach.

After I confessed my feelings to Jesus and asked him to please change *me,* I discovered that she was a very insecure person. I had actually misjudged her. She was lonely and suffering from a horrible inferiority complex. After I let down the barrier of judging, we became good friends. A few short months after that, she moved away and even after several years, we still correspond. God allowed her to work with me just long enough for me to get over my dislike for her. There is absolutely no room in any *Superniki* life for dislike, judging, or criticism.

Dale, your life can be happy in spite of the people you work with, the problems you face, and any other thorn you may have. The Bible says, "But despite all this, overwhelming victory is ours through Christ who loves us."

Dear Superniki Purple,
I understand that you're a nut about purple.
What goes with you, anyway? Purple is a
dumb color. Jim

Dear Jim,

Purple has a very special meaning to me. Purple is the color of royalty. When I became a Christian, I became a child of the *King of kings and Lord of lords*. Since I belong to Jesus, I am now royalty. Whenever I see anything purple, I am instantly reminded of my identity. No matter how many things go wrong and no matter how people may treat me, I know that I belong to Jesus Christ. I am his and he is mine!

When a girl gets married, she puts on a wedding ring. The ring is a reminder that she "belongs" to someone who loves her — her husband. It's a satisfying feeling to be real involved in something that has drained your energy and then suddenly look down and see your wedding ring. It puts a sparkle in your eyes and a warmth in your heart to be reminded that someone loves you so much that he wants to spend the rest of his life with you.

The same applies to purple. Whenever I see or wear purple, I'm reminded that Someone very special loves me! Someone very important thinks I'm worth dying for. Someone loves me every moment of the day. Someone cares about my problems and my chores. Someone is right here with me ever ready to give me strength, and help, and love. That Someone is Jesus.

Jim, I hope the next time — and every time — you see purple, you, too, will be reminded that Jesus loves you just as much as he loves me. He wants you to belong to him and to discover the joy and thrill of being royalty.

Dear Superniki Purple,
Will Jesus help me in my school work? I'm just a little kid. Ginger

Dear Ginger,

Yes, of course, Jesus will help you. I believe that Jesus will help you to relax when you have a test and that he will bring things to your memory. I don't think he will help you to the extent of cheating but he will make your mind clear of tension and fear and he will bring things to your memory that you have studied. How well I remember when I first learned this for myself. Mother was so special that I *knew* Jesus would hear her.

When I was in the seventh grade, I had the toughest, meanest arithmetic teacher! One day I had planned to spend the night with my cousin 'way out in the country. It was that day that the teacher announced that we would have a big test the next day. If I could have gotten out of going to the country, I would have. After all, there were no phones out there and how would I get in touch with Mother so that she would know to pray for my test. As soon as school was out, I ran to the phone to call Mother before the bus left. But Mother wasn't at home. Reluctantly I crawled on the bus. The excitement of staying out in the country was marred by the fear of this important test.

That night I studied extra hard but still I was worried sick about the test. I had to pray all by myself — there was no other choice; it had to be just me and God. I just had to do all right on that test and I knew that it would take his help. Looking back now, it seems almost funny that the test was so important to me.

The next day I took the test and it was even worse than I expected. All the kids talked about how hard it was. When I got home from school, I complained bitterly to Mother. Where had she been? Why hadn't she been at home when I needed her? Mother assured me that Jesus could hear my prayers. I wasn't convinced but I did quit complaining.

The following day, the teacher stood sternly before the class and gave us a severe lecture. He said that he was very disappointed in the test papers. My tummy felt kind of sick. He went on to say that most of the class had failed and that there was only one perfect grade. He was most unhappy and wasted no time in letting us know about it.

After his lecture, he began to call out names to come up and get the test papers. The first name he called was mine. Why did he have to call me first? I looked at my paper and sure enough, there was a big zero on the top of the paper. But oh, there was another zero and a one in front of them. I had made 100 — the *only* perfect score. I can't tell you how thrilled I was. God had actually heard my prayers when I had prayed all by myself!

It's quite a thrill when you first discover that the Lord is actually interested in the little things that are important to you. No matter how young or how old you are, Jesus is interested in you. He will listen to your prayers. He loves you!

Dear Superniki Purple,
There are so many decisions in the world today that I don't know which way to turn. How do you know what's important? Wesley

Dear Wesley,

It's true there are many things today that we have to decide on. Our lives are crammed full of decisions. However, there is only one decision that really matters, and that is the decision to become a Christian.

I had a brother whom I adored. Larry was quite a guy. I'm a little prejudiced, of course, but to me he was handsome, had more friends than anyone else I knew, and had personality plus. Larry graduated from Texas A&M University and was an officer in the Air Force. He loved flying and had chosen the Air Force as his career. He was married to a sweet girl and they were looking forward to the arrival of their first child. Looking at Larry at the age of twenty-three, you would have said he had the world by the tail. He had all that anyone could ask for. His family adored him, he was well educated, he loved his job and had a bright future. Why, life looked very promising for Larry. But our Heavenly Father decided that Larry's time on earth was up. Larry was killed in the jet he was piloting.

All of this that seemed so important was suddenly meaningless — worthless. What did it matter now that Larry had been handsome? What did it matter now that he had two degrees? What did it matter now that he was loved by so many? What did it matter now that he was successful? All of this now had no importance. The one and only thing that mattered was that Larry knew the Lord Jesus Christ. Nothing else counted!

As you are making your decisions, Wesley, make the only one of lasting importance — make the decision for Jesus. Remember, he loves you!

Dear Superniki Purple,

I have heard people say that you are not really saved unless you know the time and the day when you first gave your heart to the Lord. This upsets me because I can't remember.
Wanda

Dear Wanda,

I know two women whom I consider to be outstanding Christians. One lady was born of wealthy parents and lived a wicked life. After years of dope, drunkenness, three wrecked marriages, and an attempt at suicide, she found out about the love of God. After she was past fifty, she gave her heart to God. She knows the exact day and hour when her life changed.

The other lady grew up in a Christian home. When she was less than three, a metal pipe slipped from her hands and cut a chunk out of her little leg.

When her mother reached the crying child, the little one said, "I want some Jesus people." Her mother wrapped a rag around the deep cut and rushed her to the home of the best Christian available. There the kind woman picked up the child and began to rock her as the two women prayed.

After praying briefly, she asked the child if she still hurt. The child replied, "Un-huh." They prayed again and while they prayed, she fell asleep.

When she awoke, all pain had gone and did not return. Thirty years later the scar remains on her leg but better than that is the fact that the same faith in God remains with her.

When asked if she could remember when she first gave her heart to God, she replied, "I don't have any idea when I first gave my life to him but I remember the last time. I gave my life to him again today as I do every day."

Don't be upset if you can't remember the first time, Wanda. It's really not important. It's like remembering the first time your husband said, "I love you." The first time isn't as important as the last time (and I hope it was today). The same applies to being a Christian. The last time you felt God's love is the most important.

Dear Superniki Purple,

God is so busy with important matters that he can't really be bothered with our lives. Why do you think differently? Wallace

Dear Wallace,

There are too many examples for one book to hold. But I would like to give you just one tiny example. I drive almost seventy miles a day to and from work. One day I had followed a white pickup for about twenty miles. A few miles before I reached home, I changed lanes. As I did, I questioned my foolish action. I always stay in the left lane at that point because I turn left in just a few blocks. It's easier to stay in the left lane than to try to change lanes in the heavy traffic. But this day I found myself changing lanes without really thinking. There was a red light just ahead and the traffic stopped. My car was still behind the white pickup but in the next lane from it. When the light turned green, the car that had been behind me for a great distance suddenly plowed into the white pickup. The driver had seen the light change and gunned his motor without realizing that the cars in front of him had not started moving yet. If I had not changed lanes, my car would have been hit instead of the white pickup. There was quite a bit of damage but no one was seriously hurt. As I sat there motionless, I was keenly aware that it was God who had caused me to change lanes. God loves me so much that he is concerned with my health, my convenience, and my peace of mind. I know that God is interested. He has proven it over and over again.

Wallace, he is interested in you, too!

Dear Superniki Purple,

Christmas has become so commercial that it's repulsive. What happened to the real meaning of Christmas? Edna

Dear Edna,

Our Christmases are still more "Christ-centered" than you realize. So much we do has real meaning and is not just commercial nor pagan as some have said. When we give gifts, we are imitating God. When we put up a green Christmas tree, we are saying that Jesus died on a dead tree — the cross of Calvary — but he arose and lives today.

We send Merry Christmas cards and sing happy carols instead of sending unpleasant cards and singing depressing songs. Christmas is a time of "Good News!" We rejoice (spread joy) because of God's great love for us!

Lights are used everywhere. Jesus is the Light of the world. When light shines on tinsel, it's like magic. The dull tinsel actually sparkles. That is so typical of our lives. No matter how dull and ugly we are, we will become valuable and lovable when Jesus shines from within.

Christmas colors are red and green for a very good reason. Red stands for the blood of Jesus that was shed for us. Green represents life. Jesus came that we might have an abundant life. He died on the cross that we might have a happy life and be saved. "Despite all, overwhelming victory is ours through Jesus" is our promise.

Dear Superniki Purple,
Why are Christians ridiculed? It doesn't
seem fair. Charles

Dear Charles,

Most Christians are ridiculed when they do not live up to what they say they believe. I know a group of people who discuss things quite bluntly. Of this group, two of the wives "claim" to be spiritual Christians. One wife is the constant object of ridicule. When an unkind comment was repeated to me, I began to understand the reason. This woman "claims" to be a really good Christian but her actions tell a different story. Adultery is a common thing with her and getting drunk is done on the sly. While she is really active in her church and boasting of her spirituality, she is misbehaving in secret. But the secret came out and now she is the target of ridicule.

The other woman doesn't boast of being a spiritual Christian. Instead, she actually is one. People respect her because of the type of life she lives and not for what she says she believes. She is never ridiculed but is well liked and treated with the respect due a lady — and by the same ones who cruelly ridicule the other woman.

Why shouldn't the world ridicule us when we say we believe "all things work together for good to them who love God" and yet we get upset when things don't go our way? Why shouldn't we be ridiculed when we say that we have faith in God and yet we complain about everything that happens? Why shouldn't we be ridiculed when we say that we love our neighbors and yet we gossip about them? Ridicule is of our own doing.

If we are to be more like Jesus, we are to practice our religion instead of just talking it. When we do not live what we believe, our lives can't be happy. We will be victorious, happy, interesting Christians when we *practice* our religion.

There are exceptions, when people are ridiculed for what they believe even when they live it. But when you know beyond any doubt that what you believe is true, it doesn't matter what others may say. If you really know that your religion works and you have reality, unjust ridicule will not bother you at all. You should feel sorry for those who ridicule because they do not know your God.

Dear Superniki Purple,

It upsets me the way some ministers talk about the cost of being a Christian. There are so many benefits that it seems wrong to always talk about the cost. Do you agree? Fran

Dear Fran,

Yes, I do agree! I believe in the positive approach. But more than that, it seems foolish to dwell on things that aren't really all that important. I have a dear friend who is expecting a baby very soon. Can you imagine my telling her of the cost of having a baby and of being a mother? There will certainly be many physical, financial, and emotional costs involved in raising a child. However, she has made her decision to become a mother again. She has other children and has proven to be an exceptional mother. She knows about the sleepless nights, the inconveniences, the financial cost, and the emotional strain. She knows all this and yet she knows that having a precious child is worth paying the price! There is no point in telling her of the disadvantages of becoming a mother — she already knows them and is convinced that having a child is worth it all.

This is rather like being a Christian. The cost is great — it costs us our pride, our self-righteousness, our ego, our independence, our wills, and our very lives. But in its place, we receive great gifts — we receive Jesus. As he enters our lives, he furnishes us with guidance, wisdom, love, joy, and inner peace. He more than supplies every physical, financial, and emotional need. The joy of being his child is greater than any other joy.

I have shuddered as I heard mothers talk about that wonderful day when their children would be grown and out on their own. They complain of the inconveniences and the horrible growing-up stages kids go through. This reminds me of the sad Christians who live only for Heaven. Instead of enjoying God's abundant life right now, they complain and just can't wait until they get to Heaven where it will be worth it all.

Having your children grown and out on their own is a satisfaction and being in Heaven will be wonderful.

However, there is a lot of wasted time in between. The parents who enjoy their children as they grow up and don't complain about everything are much better and happier parents with better adjusted children. There is joy in being friends with your children. There is a thrill in watching them develop. It's common for parents to be excited over the first step, the first word, or the first tooth. This is like being thrilled when you first know about the Lord. The happy parent is the one who continues to be thrilled over the baseball game, the candy made, the friends acquired, the personality developing. So it is with being a Christian. It isn't enough to be happy with the Lord just on Sunday or when you first were saved. But the *Superniki Christian* is the one who finds a real thrill in knowing him every single day!

Fran, mothers don't think about the cost of being a mother when they are enjoying a precious moment with their children. I believe we as Christians should be just as thrilled over our relationship with God — even more so. We have everything to gain when we become a child of God, and so little to lose.

Dear Superniki Purple,

It's disgusting the way the younger generation has literally gone to pot. I get so sick when I read of the kids using LSD and smoking pot. What's wrong with these stupid kids?
Josie

Dear Josie,

Recently I spoke with an attractive young lady who smokes pot. As she told me of her experiences with pot, I was shocked that she would take so many risks. It seemed so foolish. She is well aware of the dangers and disadvantages of pot. I asked her what could be worth so much. She said that she smokes pot because it gives her peace. She went on to say that while under the influence of pot, nothing can upset her. She has a strange peace. Someone can chew her out or call her a filthy name and it doesn't bother her. She said that this peace varies from a few minutes to a few days.

I was sick inside as I listened to her. "Peace that passeth understanding" is available to all of us constantly and without any danger or risk. As I listened, I realized that we Christians have failed the younger generation. We have talked about God and peace and yet our lives have not reflected that peace. The kids today are too smart to accept something that we say but do not live. If we say God gives peace and yet we are constantly upset, worrying, having words with the neighbors, unhappy in the home, and miserable, they don't want any part of it. If God isn't the answer, they will look somewhere else.

Where can peace come from? There is only one answer and his name is Jesus. When he gives peace, nothing can take it away. There is one catch, though. His peace comes from a total commitment of our lives to him on a day-to-day basis. Tensions and pressures are all around us. We live in a fast world with problems of all sorts. When things begin to bug us, when people get on our nerves, it's a good sign that we have neglected our time alone with God. We often make excuses that we are too busy to be alone with God, to be recharged with his peace and love. God knows your schedule. If your time alone is while you drive down the road, mow the grass, or cook supper, God is willing to meet you more than halfway. He loves you so much that he will accept you in any position and doing most anything! He loves you so much that he wants you to have peace, in any situation. You will discover that it's worth your while to find a relationship with God.

Josie, don't condemn the kids who are frantically searching for peace. Instead, live your life with such peace and love that others will want what you have. Let the love of God so flow in your own life that you will influence the youth that you contact. Let them see in you that God is the answer. Living it has more influence than mere words. When you have real peace, others will know it — and want it.

Dear Superniki Purple,
I'm not white. Will Jesus love me, anyway?
Most white people do not even tolerate me.
What hope do I have that Jesus will? Ruthie Bell

Dear Ruthie Bell,

Just because you are not white on the outside doesn't mean that you are not white on the inside. If you have confessed your sins, "though your sins be as scarlet" he will make them white as snow. That is, of course, a figure of speech. Your sins do not have color any more than your soul has color. If you have confessed your sins, you are clean within and there is no significance to the color of the body which houses your soul. The only thing of importance to Jesus is that you have asked forgiveness of your sins.

Jesus came to all mankind. The shepherds and wisemen came to worship him as a baby. They are representatives of two distinct classes of people. The shepherds were poor and unlearned while the wisemen were well educated, with fortunes. They had something in common — Jesus.

Jesus came to all the world. That does not exclude any race, any social group, any income bracket, nor any intelligence group. Jesus loves each of us — individually.

Ruthie Bell, we should try to be like God but most of us fail miserably. Jesus loves you very, very much. He is concerned with your life. As people become more like him, they will not hate but will love. Don't judge Jesus by people. The Bible says, "For God so loved the world that he gave his only son." Ruthie Bell, the world includes you!

Dear Superniki Purple,

My married children don't ever seem to enjoy coming "home." I see them so seldom. What's the secret in getting your children to come home often? Maria

Dear Maria,

Yours is not an unusual question. I have heard more children complain about "having to go home" than I have heard say that they enjoyed going home. Those I work with tease me a lot about going home so often. They just can't understand why I would rather visit with my mother than go out and have "fun." I would like to share my mother's secret with you.

There is no getting around the generation gap. It's there and should be faced. Mother and I have the same situation that is typical in most homes. After I had been away from home for a few years, it just wasn't the same. I had my own ideas of everything from housecleaning to cooking. Mother and I didn't do anything the same way. She dressed differently, had different ideas in the home, why, she even washes dishes differently!

But my mother is an exceptional person. She recognizes the generation gap and made a point of establishing a marvelous relationship that knows no age. Of all the places in the world — bar none — I would rather go to Mother's than any other place. I find sheer delight in sitting up half the night talking with Mother. She is my very best friend and I always enjoy being with her. Why?

I am aware that my mother loves me . . . and more than that, she approves of me. That is important! I know that Mother is on my side. She never condemns nor judges me. She just loves me. When I do something wrong, she doesn't say, "Shame on you! I thought I taught you better than that!" Instead, she lovingly helps me straighten out the mess I have made and then tenderly helps me change my attitudes and hand the problem over to God. When I go home with a big problem, as I did recently, instead of feeling sorry for "her baby," she said, "Marvelous! What a golden opportunity for you to become an overcomer!" But she didn't stop there leaving me in a tight spot. We prayed together and handed the situation over to God. She encourages me and shares the goodness of the Lord with me. There is absolutely nothing more interesting than talking about the Lord and listening to someone share the reality of knowing God.

Instead of feeling responsible for everything I do, she shows interest, concern, and genuine love, knowing that I am *God's* responsibility.

Maria, if you want your children to come home often, accept the fact that they are no longer children. Don't preach at them nor pity them. Instead of complaining and feeling sorry for yourself, let them feel your love and approval. Listen with interest to whatever they are talking about. Then bring God into your relationship. Share your faults and experiences with your children. Let them become a part of you. Don't try to be perfect. Let them know that you are human and that you love them. The more they enjoy your company, the more effort they will make to visit you.

Dear Superniki Purple,

Do you believe in equal rights? If so, don't you believe that Ephesians 5:24 is out dated and antiquated? Phyllis

Dear Phyllis,

Ephesians 5:24 says, "Therefore as the church is subject unto Christ, so let the wives be to their husbands in everything." I tested this Scripture for myself and found amazing results. Space will permit only two examples.

The first time I remember ever going to church with my dad was at my own wedding. Several years later, he agreed to start going to church with us but only to the church of his choice. Since he was not an active Christian, my mother should (?) have had the right to choose her own church. But she didn't, because she believes the Bible. Dad didn't pick a church in town but a small church 'way out in the country. It was an inconvenience to get there, and yet through the years of attending that little church we have received the real joy of loving Jesus.

Can I say Dad was just being stubborn? Of course not! Jesus was leading Dad in making that decision. You see, Jesus is smarter than my dad and anyone else.

The same Scripture proved applicable in my own marriage. One Sunday Don was eager to get back to Houston. When we got in from church, I wanted to stop and eat but Don was in such a hurry that he said, "No." The normal reaction for me should have been to demand that he feed me rather than drive two hours home in the heat of the day without eating. But I realized that if I want to become *Superniki,* then I had better start putting the Scriptures into practice.

And so without any argument, I said, "Okay." When we went by his parents' home, his mother had just finished cooking our favorite dishes. Immediately we sat down to a real feast. Later I asked Don if he knew that his mother was preparing lunch for us. He said that he didn't know — but God did.

There are numerous other incidents that have given me such joy in letting Don make the decisions and not demanding my own "equal rights." God is bigger and smarter than I. If he designed life with the man as the boss — as long as he does not conflict with the Bible — then who am I to say that God was wrong?

Dear Superniki Purple,

What does God have against people having money? Jesus said it would be very difficult for rich people to serve him. Why? Candy

Dear Candy,

Jesus was well aware of our human nature. In America most of us could be considered "rich" in comparison to our forefathers. We have so much materially and yet we have so little gratitude. We were created to praise God. We take so much for granted. We give ourselves credit for earning so much. We tend to leave God out of the picture altogether.

For instance, do you give God credit for your electricity or do you complain because your monthly bill is rather high? Do you ever stop and think what it would be like to have no electricity? Can you perhaps remember your grandmother's house before she had electricity? Remember how thankful everyone was when they first had it? Now we take it for granted. It hasn't been too many years since you had to warm your feet with a heated iron wrapped in cloths. Now most people have central heat or electric blankets. After the first few winters, even those are taken for granted. Praise God for everyday things? We expect to have so much and yet we fail to praise God for any of it.

Buying your first car was probably an important event in your life. As a Christian, you probably thanked the Lord for transportation. Now that you have had many cars and you consider them a necessity, do you still praise God for your car? The car you have right now is probably much more expensive than the first one you owned. Why has the praise gone? It's gone because we are too "rich."

You get the point, Candy. We are greedy people. The more we get, the more we must have. We are so greedy that we work, work, work for more, more, more instead of appreciating what we have. The secret of a happy life is to praise God for the many blessings we have. When Jesus said that it would be difficult for the rich, he knew that we would be selfish and greedy. He wasn't saying that we weren't to have enough so that we may help others. He has promised to supply all our needs. He was speaking of the hindrance of being "rich" because he knew we would feel independent — we wouldn't sense our need of God.

Candy, think about it. Don't you have a lot to be thankful for? Aren't you blessed with many things?

Praise and thanksgiving are not duties — they are pleasures. When a continual praise is in your heart, your life will be satisfying. You will not be like the "rich" of whom Jesus spoke. As you praise him, you are acknowledging your need of him. He has promised to inhabit our praises. Do you want God with you constantly? If so, praise him and he is right with you!

Dear Superniki Purple,

If I get saved on my deathbed, I'll go to Heaven. Why should I get saved now? What is the advantage? Steve

Dear Steve,

It's true that you will go to Heaven if you get saved moments before you die. The sad part will be that you will have lived your entire life without the bonus of God's love and guidance.

If I had waited until my deathbed to get married, I would not have died an "old maid." That's about all you could say for my marriage. I would have missed all the joys of marriage.

Even if I had waited until now to get married, I would have lost a dozen years of "belonging" to someone who loves me. I would have been on my own to take care of myself and perhaps be lonely. I would have missed the comfort and joy of marriage. But getting married now would be much better than waiting until my deathbed. I would still have the rest of my life to look forward to and to enjoy sharing the happiness of marriage.

This, multiplied by a million, is what it is like to wait until your deathbed to find out about the love of God. You'll make it to Heaven but you will have lived years without the countless advantages of belonging to God. To be more specific, you would have to rely completely on your own intelligence, your own judgment, and your own abilities. While you are probably a sharp fellow, you can't compete with God!

Steve, the advantages are too great to pass up! Why would you want to wait and take a chance on barely getting to Heaven? Since you are a "thinker," don't settle for anything less than the very best. And the best is knowing God for yourself!

Dear Superniki Purple,

I don't have any patience and yet I can't pray for patience because I'm afraid something dreadful will happen to me. I guess I just don't understand what patience is. Colleen

Dear Colleen,

Patience is defined by Webster as "calmness in waiting for something to happen." You want to be calm and peaceful, don't you? Then you want patience. Patience is actually complete trust in God — with no reservations.

If you tell your son to be home at midnight, you will either trust him and wait patiently for midnight or you will fret and worry, wondering if he'll make it home by then. If you have faith in him, you will not become upset as midnight draws near. If you don't trust him, you will become more uneasy and unhappy the later it gets.

The same applies to God. If you trust God completely, then patience will come naturally. If you turn a particular situation or person over to God, if you believe God hears your prayers and loves you enough to answer, you will have infinite patience as you trust God's timing in solving the problem. However, if you doubt that God is concerned about you and your problems, then you will begin to worry, fret, and try to "help" God solve the problem. It is only when we realize that God cares about the details that make up our lives that we are able to relax and trust him. Then God is free to guide us and lead us in the way that is best for all concerned.

Patience is the quality of being sure. You can be sure of God! He exists, and he loves you, and he is capable of handling any problem that you may have.

Dear Superniki Purple,

I'm a grandmother with a heavy heart. I have just discovered that my father wasn't really my father at all. I'm so hurt that no one ever told me the truth. I feel unworthy and unloved. I wouldn't ask my mother any details because she is quite elderly and my questions might kill her. I hate myself for having lived a lie all these years. What can I do?
Gerrie

Dear Gerrie,

I'm sure your discovery has been a shock to you. However, do not place too much emphasis on something that happened so long ago. If you are a grandmother, your childhood is behind you. Was it a pleasant one? Be glad! If it was unpleasant, forget it. The only thing that matters now is the identity of your real Father. I am not speaking of your earthly father but of your Heavenly Father. If you know God as your Father, that is all that really is important. Place your emphasis there. If you are his child, you are entitled

to be loved and happy and know that you
are wanted.

The Bible says that all things work together
for good. "All" is a very inclusive word and
includes your birth. Forgive your parents for
whatever they did wrong and for whatever situation they found themselves in. Then forgive your mother for concealing the truth
from you. Put the best interpretation on her
actions. Instead of feeling resentment or hate,
realize that she was trying to protect you from
something unpleasant. Realize that she loved
you so much that she tried to protect you.
Most of all, forgive her as God has forgiven
you of your mistakes.

As to your "living a lie," this is, of course,
not the case at all. To live a lie, you would
have to have known the truth about your par-
entage and then have tried to deceive others
deliberately. Since the circumstances were not
known to you, you certainly could not have
participated in any deception!

The Bible says, "Acknowledge him in all
your ways." If you have had unusual circumstances, God will use them to mold you into
his perfect pattern for your life. Everything
that happened to you is part of God's plan
for your life. You can trust God to work out
your life for your good. He has promised that
he will . . . and he *will!*

Dear Superniki Purple,

Is God really interested in the tiny things that make up our lives? I can't see it myself.
Richard

Dear Richard,

God's interest in us is more than we can comprehend. Don took our fathers on a long trip one weekend. We agreed to meet at my sister's house the following Sunday. Then our parents would go home and we would go on to our home some thirty miles away. They didn't have a key to Bonnie's house and so it was agreed that the back door would be left unlocked if we were not there.

However, in the confusion, the door was locked and we all met at church — the ladies, that is. The mothers and I arrived just as Sunday school started. As soon as it was over, I asked Bonnie if the men had made it in. She said that she thought the plans had been changed and so she had left the house locked. Panic! I quickly left the church and rushed to her house. I knew that the men would have

had little or no sleep and that they would be
tired and a little upset if they found a locked
house. As I turned the corner on her street,
the men were just getting out of the car. The
timing could not have been more perfect! I
unlocked the house, welcomed them home,
and made it back to church in time for the
sermon.

If we had figured and refigured, we could
not have timed our meeting so perfectly. They
had driven more than a thousand miles and
I had driven only one mile and yet the timing was perfect. God was aware of the physical condition of the tired men. He allowed
the door to be locked so that I would have
to know that God cares about me and those
I love. He wants to prove himself and his
concern to me. So often we just shrug off
such "coincidences." When you belong to
God, nothing can happen unless God allows
it and arranges it.

Dear Superniki Purple,

My preschool-age child is a nervous wreck. The doctor says he is developing emotional problems. My own ulcer is driving me nuts because I feel so helpless. What can I do? Please help. Eloise

Dear Eloise,

We have been slow in recognizing that small children are affected by the emotions and attitudes of the adults with whom they come in contact — especially their parents. I have a friend whose little boy broke out in a severe case of hives. They could not find any cause for them. After discussing it at length, the parents realized that the hives appeared after they themselves had had quite an argument and were not even on speaking terms. The tension and discord in the home had greatly affected the child.

Children copy our examples. They don't do as we say to do — they do as we do. If you are a nervous wreck, confused, unhappy, worrying about anything, then your child has little hope of escaping that same state of mind. If you and your husband quarrel, the tension will be felt by your children. The sad part is that the effect will go with them throughout life — not just for a few minutes. You and your husband may settle your difference, but your children will not clear their emotions as easily.

There is a marvelous solution, though! His name is Jesus! When you become really acquainted with him, you will be a different person and a much better parent. You cannot trust in him and still worry about anything. You cannot realize how much he loves you and still be unhappy. You cannot feel the presence of the Lord in your home and have discord at the same time. When you have a disagreement with your husband, instead of getting into a heated argument that ends with neither of you speaking, you will discuss it, pray about it, and reach a solution. If you have to give in more than you feel that you should, you will take this complaint to Jesus and he will give you peace and make you willing to go the second mile. He will give you a forgiving spirit and a love and respect for your husband and your children. That kind of security is priceless and will give your child such emotional strength that it will take something pretty upsetting to get the best of him.

Eloise, the best thing you can do for your child is to dedicate your own life to God and to allow his love to flow through you to your family. Give him control of your life and allow him to give you peace that will be passed on to your child. That's the very best medicine anywhere!

Dear Superniki Purple,

I have everything that I could want to make me happy and yet I never seem to be satisfied. There is definitely something missing in my life and I don't know what it is. Is anyone ever really content? Sallye

Dear Sallye,

When God made us, he designed our "heart" in a most unusual manner. He deliberately left out a small portion of it that could only be filled by him. The effect on us is the same as having a cavity in a tooth. When there's a hole, it's miserable until it's filled.

If you try to fill it with a piece of food, it really smarts! If you put cotton in it, it still hurts when the cotton gets wet. Everything that you put in it will hurt until it's what the dentist orders — a filling prepared just for that cavity.

In much the same manner, we try to fill the cavity in our hearts. We try to satisfy our inner longing with success, popularity, money, marriage, and countless other "good" things. For a short time whatever we have substituted may satisfy. But it's like some of the transplants doctors are doing now. For a short time they work. Then the rest of the body rejects them. So it is with the heart. Soon the body rejects the substitute for God in our heart. The old longing and dissatisfaction returns.

Since God created you, he knew what he was doing. There is nothing that can take the place of him in your heart. But the gap in your heart cannot be filled just once and then be forgotten. When God comes into your life, there is joy and peace. However, if God does not have a part in your daily life, soon you feel the same old emptiness. We must be constantly aware of our need for God and his great love for us! When you have God, you have the only true contentment!

Dear Superniki Purple,

My son-in-law whips my precious grandson so severely that he has bruises. It breaks my heart. I have tried to reason with him but this only makes him mad and he shouts, "My kid is going to mind." What can I do? Granny

Dear Granny,

Discipline is necessary in any child's life. However, there is quite a difference between discipline and brutal whippings. Your son-in-law wants his son to turn out better than he was. He expects too much of the child and the least little failure on the child's part brings out the fear in him that his child will be like him — a failure. His own insecurity causes him to react violently to the child's behavior. When a parent has security and love (and is happy with himself), he will not become so upset with his child's faults. Instead, with loving understanding he will correct him. It's the confused, frustrated, insecure parent who spanks the child until it becomes a whipping. The child has to suffer for the mixed-up emotions of the parent. It's the father who needs help.

That's where you come in. When you add to his problems by your feelings of contempt and disapproval (although justified), you are only making things worse for the child. The father's pride will not let him stop whipping the child because that would be an admission that he was wrong again.

Granny, you can help by praying — with the right attitudes — for the father. He needs help — more help than any human being can give. The only solution is God. The father needs to know that God loves him no matter what a mess he's made of his life. When he learns of God's love, he will be able to accept himself. Then it will be much easier for him to discipline his child properly.

Praying with love is powerful. The Bible says "God is love." As you pray with love the results will amaze you. When you love the "sick" father as you would a physically sick person, you will find it easy to pray for him. As you do, you will notice a change in him. God answers prayer!

Dear Superniki Purple,

My husband has just been offered a nice promotion with one unpleasant stipulation. He will have to move to a distant city. I don't want to move! I have a gorgeous house which I adore. I live near my family and friends. I don't want to move! I have cried, begged, pleaded, but he is all set on moving. What am I going to do? Robbin

Dear Robbin,

I know a lady who lived in the same city to which you are moving. They had a fabulous house. Her husband was transferred before the house sold. She stayed behind to sell it. She resented moving and was rather ugly about it. They were moving to a small town with no hope of finding anything to compare with the dream house they had. In the three weeks that she lived in the house alone, she changed her sense of values and the rest of her life.

That gorgeous house didn't mean anything when her husband wasn't with her. He was what made the house a home. She discovered that being with him and making him happy was much more important than living in a fabulous house.

At this moment, you are at the crossroads of your marriage. The way you behave in the next few weeks will have a definite bearing on your future. If you prove to be the kind of wife that every man dreams of, you will not wallow in self-pity and feel as though you are being punished. Realize that your husband is doing all of this because he loves you. He doesn't relish moving any more than you do. It's no fun to look for another house, change jobs, work with people you don't even know, accept more responsibility, face unseen problems, especially when you add the task of pacifying an unhappy wife! He wants to make a better living for you and your family. He loves you and wants the best for you.

Besides, be realistic; has your crying and begging done any good? I doubt that it has done any more than make your husband unhappy. You're still moving, aren't you? Then accept the fact that the decision has been made. Be mature enough to accept it and then start out with expectation and love. Be so happy that your husband will actually look forward to spending the rest of his life with such a marvelous wife!

We tend to get what we expect. If you leave down in the dumps and convinced that it's the end of the world, you are asking for trouble. Expect to find an interesting new life in your new location. Expect to make your husband so happy that he'll be extra glad he married you. What have you got to lose? "The future is as bright as the promises of God!"

Dear Superniki Purple,
I think Easter eggs are pagan. Why do the churches sponsor such things? It just doesn't seem right. Zelda

Dear Zelda,

Easter eggs are a lovely symbol of our lives as Christians. If you will watch an Easter egg hunt, you will notice that all of the children are excited, happy, and filled with enthusiasm. They know that there are "treasures" waiting for them if they will just look for them. They don't know exactly where they are nor what they will be. They may find candy eggs or real ones of bright colors. Sometimes the Easter eggs are hollow, hiding extra special treasures within. Each egg is a delight to find and a delight to have. Occasionally the going gets pretty rough and a little child may lose hope but just as he is ready to give up, he finds another little egg and all of the enthusiasm comes right back. Each child goes in a different direction to find his "treasure." When the Easter egg hunt is over, all the children gather around and talk about what they found, and where. There are always enough eggs to go around so no one is left out. There is happy conversation as they share their discoveries.

Our lives as Christians are much like the Easter egg hunt. When we become children of God, we are filled with great expectations. We expect the Lord to fulfill the many wonderful promises that are given to us in the Bible. We expect to find thrilling experiences in serving the Lord. We don't know what we will receive, but we know that everything the Lord has in store for us is good — and for our good. Occasionally life gets dull and uninteresting and we think maybe we're missing out and we should just quit trying. But just about then the Lord blesses us in a special way, uses us to help someone else, or answers a prayer. Immediately we regain our enthusiasm and are thrilled by Jesus. The Bible says "Seek and ye shall find; knock and the door shall be opened to you." As we seek God's best, we will receive.

When a group of Christians get together, it's like the kids after an Easter egg hunt. We all gather round and tell about the good things the Lord is doing. When people are talking about the goodness and provision of God, the conversation is happy and interesting. There is real joy in serving the Lord and in sharing our experiences with others.

The only real satisfaction is Jesus. When you find him, you have found the *real treasure!* When you have Jesus, you have everything!

Dear Superniki Purple,
   My children are as stubborn as any kids could be. It upsets me because I can't seem

to change them. What should I do? They are worse than any mule. Pat

Dear Pat,

To be as stubborn as a mule is more of a compliment than an insult! I took a tour down into the Grand Canyon once. The trail is very narrow and winding and often on the edge of a steep cliff. When you are up on top of the mule, it seems as though you could easily plunge into the canyon below. It's a frightening experience.

As I admitted my fears to our trail guide, he informed me that there had never been an accident caused by a mule. The mule is so stubborn that he will not take one step forward without smelling the ground in front of him. If a rock falls into the trail, the mule smells of it carefully before proceeding. It doesn't matter if the mule ahead of him continues, each mule will stop and smell of the rock for himself. The mule won't take your word for it if you try to coax him on. The mule is so stubborn that he is going to find out for himself.

It seems that stubbornness in the right place becomes steadfastness. If we are just stubborn for the sake of being stubborn, hopefully we will outgrow it. But when we have been stubborn all our lives, it seems that we won't take anyone's word for anything important — we have to know for ourselves. When you are stubborn and someone tells you that it's exciting to be a Christian, you don't dilly-dally around and think that maybe you'll try it when you're old and there is nothing better to do. Instead, you are so stubborn that you decide that you are going to see for yourself if it really works — if there really is something to being a Christian. Then, once you try it, you find such a thrill and satisfaction in being a child of God that no one and no situation can get you to change your mind. Again your stubbornness takes over and you wouldn't budge for anyone or anything.

Once you realize what a "good thing" being a Christian really is, nothing can sway you. Then no matter how rough things get, no matter how scary the road, no matter what may come or go, you can plod on with a mule-like assurance that you will get there safely.

Pat, don't worry if your children are stubborn. As children they are just beginning to learn about steadfastness. You want them to grow up finding out things for themselves. You wouldn't want them to just accept your religion. You want them to find out about God for themselves.

Dear Superniki Purple,

I can't go with you on this religious kick you are on. Why don't you promote "free love"? Sex is a lot more interesting than religion and you'd have a lot more people interested in what you are saying. Who cares about dull, uninteresting religion? Gordon

Dear Gordon,

A friend of mine once said, "If there is anything better than sex, the good Lord must have kept it for himself." At first this annoyed me because it seemed sacrilegious. I resented the "lowering" of God's great love to the standards of sex as we think of it today. As I was stewing about his smarty remark, I asked God to please show me the value of his love and to teach me the real difference between God's love and physical love.

Sex is great — I'm not knocking it. God created us perfectly. He gave us a sexual love to express the depths of love to our spouse. This is sacred and wonderful.

But let me tell you about the "anything better"! There is a "feeling," a "satisfaction," a "joy" that so far surpasses sex that it seems to degrade the emotion and the contentment to talk about it at the same time you speak of sex. You have heard that God loves you. It probably went in one ear and out the other without having any real meaning to you. It isn't something that would grab you like thinking that Miss America loves you or Miss Sexpot is turned on by you. The knowledge of God's love is something that has to sink into your heart.

For years I had sung the song "Jesus Loves Me" but it took a long time for me to really grasp the true meaning. One night Mother and I were praying about a pressing problem. After we had prayed, we were silent as we listened for the Lord to speak to us in any manner he chose. Presently I heard a very clear voice coming from behind me. The voice said, "Have I not said, ye have not because ye ask not?" As he spoke, the room was filled with the sweetest presence of love. We could not see God but his presence was felt in the kitchen as we listened.

The unusual part came the next morning. A visiting minister was speaking at our church. The sermon was good and uplifting. One of the Scriptures he read was, "Ye have not be-

cause ye ask not." Mother and I grinned at
each other as if to say that God was confirm-
ing what he had said the night before. This
made us feel good.

After the service the visiting minister asked
to speak to me. He asked if that Scripture
meant anything special to me. When he started
to read *that* Scripture, the Lord spoke to him
about me. I had never met this minister before. He was eager to know what the Scripture meant to me. I was overjoyed! I was
filled with appreciation and love and shock
that God loved me so much that he would
allow a stranger to ask me about the same
Scripture that God had spoken to me the night
before! When I told the minister, he rejoiced
with me.

There is nothing with which we can mea-
sure this kind of love. The knowledge that I
am important to God has put a contentment
in my heart that I did not know was possible.
I find myself grinning without any outward
reason. Nothing can be as exciting as really
knowing that God loves me as an individual.

Comparing God's love to sexual love, I am
surprised at how little we know of love. I'm
not against sex. But it can't begin to compare
nor take the place of God's love.

Gordon, you know about sexual love. If
you think that's something, wait till you dis-

cover God's love! When it becomes a reality to you, you will agree with me that God's love is superlative. It's Heavenly!

Dear Superniki Purple,

Can God lead us without our knowledge? I have asked him to but I don't know whether he does or not. Hap

Dear Hap,

If you have asked God to lead you, he has! Now you should ask God to let you know *how* he has led you. This is so thrilling that everyone should have it proven to them at least once. You will be so thrilled that your faith will increase immensely.

At one point I was a little discouraged because I couldn't see that God had any control over my life. I kept praying that God would show me something — anything — that would prove that he had control of me.

One Sunday someone mentioned a man
who used to attend our Bible study. We
passed a sign that he had painted and someone just mentioned his name. The next day I
thought of him again and decided that I'd
drop him a note to tell him that we had
missed him in our Bible study. He hadn't
been there in four months. So Monday I sent
him a little card which had the poem, "I've
never seen God but I know how I feel; it's
people like you who make him so real," on
the front of it. I told him that we had missed
his inspiring comments and we all hoped that
he would be back soon. On Tuesday I mailed
the card and promptly forgot all about it.

Thursday night the man came to our house.
It was the first time he had ever been there.
He had to come by and tell us what had happened. Wednesday he just hit bottom. He
said that every time he tried to do something
for the Lord or say something to someone, it
was taken wrongly, and he looked rather foolish, and nothing was going right. He, too, had
been complaining to the Lord that no one
was understanding what he was trying to say
and so he told the Lord that he was shutting
up. He would be a silent Christian from now
on. He was just going to stop telling others
about the excitement of being a Christian. If
he didn't get bawled out, he got cussed out, or

ignored, or something. He told the Lord that he had just *had* it. He said he was as discouraged as he could be . . . until. . . . When he got home that day, there was my card saying what an inspiration he had been to me and all of the others who had been in the Bible study. He said that I would never know what that card meant to him nor how it lifted his spirits.

When I replied, "Isn't the Lord good?" it suddenly hit me. What did I mean casually saying, "Isn't the Lord good?" How exciting! The Lord knew ahead of time that this man would need encouraging and so he let my note be delayed four months until just the very day that it was needed. I didn't write him because I'm a nice gal. Nor did I write because I should invite him to the Bible study. Why should I invite him back? I wrote him because the Lord knew that he needed encouragement. I had nothing at all to do with the timing. The Lord timed it.

It's easy to look back and see it all now. I'm not smart enough to know when someone is going to be in need of encouraging — but God is.

Hap, ask God to show you — at least once — and your faith and enthusiasm will increase so that you will find a new joy in being his.

Dear Superniki Purple,
I know I ought to pray but it seems so point-less. Why bother? Joyce

Dear Joyce,

We have an automatic mental block against anything that we feel we "ought to" do. Prayer is no different. If I told you that I have a job for you that is nothing more than plugging cords into electrical sockets, you wouldn't be the slightest bit interested. It sounds so dull and pointless that you wouldn't take the job because you would be bored to pieces. However, if I approached you in an-other manner, perhaps your answer would be different. If I said, "When you go home to-night, your home will be very dark, hot and stuffy. The Texas heat will have made your house like an oven. You're going to be mis-erable. But if you will 'plug in' this cord into an electrical socket, lights will come on and the creepiness of darkness will disappear. The lights will make your home more cheerful and you will be able to see what you are doing.

Now 'plug in' this cord and the air conditioner will come on and you will enjoy the coolness. If you are hungry, 'plug in' this cord and you will be able to prepare a delicious meal on your electric stove. If you want to be entertained, 'plug in' this cord and the color TV will come on for your enjoyment." Of course I could go on and on and on. When you stop and think about it, perhaps it isn't such a bad job after all. In fact, I *like* the idea of just "plugging in" a cord and enjoying the many advantages of electricity. It certainly changes things around a house, doesn't it!

Prayer is much the same. It sounds like Dullsville when all you think of is tossing prayers into the Heavens. Prayer is the cord that connects us to the source of power — the Generator — Jesus. When we are connected to him, the Scripture says, "With God, *nothing* is impossible!" This will become a reality to you. When we "plug in" to Jesus, a drab life can be turned into something exciting and wonderful, and disappointments can turn into peace of mind. Jesus is the Light of the world — all darkness must go. When the world seems dark and lonely and unhappy, all we have to do is "plug in" to Jesus and he will make the future seem right again. He will put enthusiasm into our lives. Jesus died on

the cross that we might have an abundant life
— that doesn't mean a life filled with unhappiness and defeat. We are to be *Superniki*. Jesus paid the price on Calvary in order that
we might *live* and not just exist.

If you haven't discovered the excitement of
prayer, you are missing the greatest thrill in
all the world. There is nothing to compare
with the thrill of being in his presence.

Try prayer — it works!

Dear Superniki Purple,

*I would like to give my life to God but I
just don't know how. This may sound silly but
I really don't know what I am supposed to do.
How does God take my heart? I have confessed my sins and told him that I want to be
a Christian — what now?* Tony

Dear Tony,

Suppose I came to see you with a nice
gift. When I arrived, I put the gift on the table and said, "Tony, I brought you some-

thing. It's on the table." Then we had a nice visit and I left. It's entirely up to you whether or not you take the gift. I have done all that I have to do. I have told you that I have a gift for you on the table. You have to go to the table and take the gift and do whatever you choose with the gift. That's simple, isn't it!

It's just as simple when we give our hearts and lives to God. In prayer we say, "God, here I am. I want to give my life to you. I want you to control my life and my thoughts and my actions. Please." The rest is up to God. He will take your heart and life. You have done all that you have to do — you have laid your life on the altar.

We try to make something difficult out of something very easy. When I brought you the gift, I didn't tell you what to do with it nor take it back home with me. Once given to you, it was yours to keep. Once we give our lives to God, we aren't supposed to turn right around and tell him what to do with it nor what we will or won't do nor who will or won't like it. When we give our lives to God, it must be lock, stock, and barrel.

You know how happy it makes you to give a nice gift to someone you love. How much happier you will be when you give your life to Someone who loves you so much. When

God takes your life, you will find an excitement and peace that you never knew possible.

Tony, ask him to take your life — and he will. He knows how.

Dear Superniki Purple,

Some people never seem to have a care in the world. It's disgusting that they can be so happy when there are so many things that we should worry about. Patti

Dear Patti,

Don has a favorite expression which is "no sweat." Whenever he calls me at work, he always wants to know how I'm doing. If I don't sound enthusiastic because I'm pushed with too much work, or something is bothering me, or things are going wrong, he will ask, "Is the Lord good?" There is no way that I can say "No." I know beyond any doubt that the Lord is better than just good. So I have to smile and say "Yes." Then his standard reply is, "Okay; no sweat!"

This means that if we know that the Lord is good then nothing else can cause us to worry or fret. If we know that God cares about us and our lives, then what is there to be upset about? If we know that God loves us, then what does it matter if others are unkind?

Patti, if you are sure — really sure — 'way down deep in your heart that God is your Father and he loves you, then "no sweat" can be your motto, too. When he is on your side, nothing else matters. You and God are more than a match for any situation. When he is yours and you are his, you will have a song in your heart.

Patti, "no sweat." God loves you!

Dear Superniki Purple,

Some Scriptures really irritate me. Why should God demand that we should love him only, and why do we have to give so much? That doesn't sound like a good God. Surely you can't have an answer for this. Ben

Dear Ben,

At first glance, it does seem that God is a little selfish and self-centered but that's only because you haven't tried to understand his reasoning for those Scriptures and because you don't understand how very much he loves you.

The Bible tells us that we must not lean on our own understanding and I really can see why. It isn't that God is so self-centered that he can't stand the competition of our having other gods. It's not that way at all.

It is that God loves us so much that he wants only the best for us. He doesn't want us to settle for anything less than the best, either. It is easy to make money our "god." Now none of us are going to worship money in the way that we normally think of worship. But there are many people who put all their emphasis on money. They figure as long as they have money, they have the world by the tail. Now the Lord knew all about this kind of thinking and that's why he said, "You shall have no other gods before me." He doesn't want us to become so wrapped up in thinking that money is the solution to everything that we will begin to worship money. So what's wrong with money? Nothing! We all need it and must have it. The wrong comes from thinking that money can solve all our problems. That is placing the emphasis on money instead of God. The sad but true fact is that money can disappear suddenly for so many reasons. You may fool yourself into thinking that you are such a good manager that your money could never run out.

God doesn't want us to be poor — far from it. As long as we keep money in the right perspective, I believe he will allow us to have more than enough. He has promised to supply all our needs. But he won't give it to us just so we can brag about how much money we have.

The Bible says that it is more blessed to give than to receive. When he gives us money, we are expected to spread it around — to give to others — to help his cause — to help his people. It really is true that you receive much more joy in giving than in receiving. Giving doesn't apply only to money. A kind word, a smile, a simple deed, or a bit of encouragement given in love will be a joy to give as well as to receive. I have discovered that I enjoy saying sweet things that I really mean to people almost as much as they enjoy hearing them. When I see someone respond, I am happy.

Ben, God knew what he was doing when he said that we should have no other gods before him. He wants us to know that the only real value is in him . . . the only real security is in him . . . and the only real happiness is in him. When he told us that we should give, he wanted us to discover the thrill of giving. It really is fun when done from the heart. Why don't you try it and find out for yourself?

Dear Superniki Purple,

I live in horror that my mother will die before I do. I couldn't go on without her. How can I get over this nightmare I find myself living in? Josie

Dear Josie,

That has a familiar ring to it. Many times I have felt the same way, and for years I lived with a nagging fear that my mother would die first. My mother is an exceptional person and my dearest friend. For years I had nightmares about her dying and they always left me with an ache 'way down deep inside.

She knew how I felt about her dying. So we teased and I would tell her that I prayed that I would die first because I wouldn't want to live without her. Mother would just laugh and never take me very seriously. We both knew that we have no control over death nor who would die first. One day as I reminded Mother that I just had to die first, it hit me what I was saying. What a liar I was! In one breath I was saying that I loved Mother with all my heart and yet in the very next breath I was saying that I wanted to die first. Mother had already lost two of her four children. If I really love her, I would not want her to have to go through the heartbreak of losing another child. If someone must have pain, if someone must suffer, I would rather it be me.

Fortunately, neither of us has died yet. So what am I going to do about it? I have no guarantee that I will live this day through — nor have you. Therefore, first of all, I will make certain that everything is right between me and God. Then I will go to Mother and tell her exactly how I feel about her. I do love her and I tell her so — often. The ambition of my life is to live every day as though it were my last — it really could be, you know. That would mean that I would treat everyone I meet with the same love and kindness that I would if I knew for sure that I would not live another day or that he would not live another day.

Josie, love your mother and let her know that you do. Then acknowledge that God always knows best. If she should die before you do, be glad that you can take her place in the heartache. Love her enough.

Dear Superniki Purple,

There are times when I'm so restless that I don't know what to do. I'm not happy and yet there is nothing I can pinpoint that makes me unhappy. Marcella

Dear Marcella,

I was riding in a lovely new car with some of the people I love most in all the world. It was a most enjoyable drive until the driver stopped in a "no parking zone" to go into a store. Suddenly everything changed. The seats were just as comfortable, the atmosphere just as nice, and the people just as lovable, and yet I changed. The peace and joy that had been mine left and I was filled with apprehension and mixed emotions. I didn't know whether to stay in the back seat or to get out and move the car, or sit behind the wheel in case the police came, or just what. The driver was in the store only a minute and yet it seemed like an hour. I was miserable. When he returned we moved out of the "no parking zone" and things returned to normal. Once again I was happy and enjoyed the company of those I love. But I wasn't, so as long as we were out of the will of the law.

Jesus paid the price for us to have a good life. With salvation he also paid for peace and happiness. However, if there comes a time when we get out of the will of the Lord, we get in a "no parking zone," so to speak. When we are not where we should be, tension, worry, and anxieties take over.

Marcella, we can never be truly happy until God is in complete control of our lives.

When he is in charge, happiness naturally follows.

Dear Superniki Purple,

I hear people talk about their sweet, thoughtful husbands and it just makes me sick. My husband is a decent man and a good father and yet he doesn't waste any words on sweet talk. Does this mean he doesn't really love me?
Alda

Dear Alda,

One of the most important lessons anyone must learn is the importance of interpretation. First Corinthians 13 says, "Love puts the very best interpretation on everything."

We seldom say what we really mean. When a mother says, "Eat your carrots, Lisa," she is not saying "I don't like you so I am forcing you to eat something you do not enjoy." We know that the mother is really saying, "Lisa, I love you very much and I want to see you healthy and happy. I know that if you will learn to eat the foods that are good for you, you will be healthy, and happiness will be easier."

We have also learned that when someone says that you have on a pretty dress or a good-looking suit, what they are really saying to you is, "Let's be friends. I like you." But since we don't have the nerve to come right out and say, "I like you," we try to find some less obvious way of saying it.

The fact that your husband works hard and tries to earn a good living for you means that he loves you. The fact that he comes home at night instead of heading for the nearest bar means that he enjoys your company. When he buys a new appliance for you, he's saying that he loves you and wants to make your housework as easy as possible. When he wants you to go places with him, he's saying that he loves you and is proud to be seen with you.

Most husbands grow up without hearing the sweet words that you want to hear. If you want to hear sweet things, then you condition him by telling him the same things you want to hear. Sweet talk works both ways, you know. The fact that you've been married ten or fifteen years makes no difference. He still has an ego and would like to know that you are still glad you married him. He would like to know that you are proud of him. He would like to know the simple basic truth that you love him. Often we wives expect our husbands to bend over backwards pleasing us and yet we ignore the fact that it has to work two ways.

If you never tell your husband that you love him, why should he bother telling you that he loves you? When your husband hears you saying sincere, sweet things day after day, he is bound to get the message. When you are a sweet, loving, and forgiving wife, you are setting an example before him that he will probably follow. It's worth a try, anyway.

Dear Superniki Purple,

I don't have any luck with having my prayers answered. Why should I bother praying when I never see results? It seems like a waste of time and besides, it's discouraging.
Billie

Dear Billie,

If you pray and nothing happens, then you should change your method of praying. I have discovered an amazing secret that I would like to pass on to you. It's so exciting and it really works. There is a simple procedure to follow when you pray.

Be specific. Don't just pray in generalities. If you really want something, what is it and why? When you know for sure what you want, decide if it would be pleasing to the Lord for you to get what you ask for.

Base it on a Scripture. Look for a Scripture that promises you whatever you are praying for. My favorite Scripture along these lines is, "He will give you the desires of your heart." I believe that means that God will put the desire in your heart and then he will fulfill that desire. Remember that his desires cannot conflict with other teachings in the Bible. God never contradicts himself.

Believe. Matthew 21:22: "And all things, whatsoever ye shall ask in prayer, *believing,* ye shall receive." This is the magic to prayer. Too often we pray without faith. We don't expect God to answer our prayers. We pray and yet we do not believe. If you really believe that God exists, that God will hear your prayer, that God loves you enough to answer your prayer, and you are praying in accordance with his will, you will not ask in vain.

Praise him. After you have told God your desire, your request, or your aim, then begin immediately to thank him for the answer. It may take a long time to get what you have prayed for. That should not change your mode of praying. Anytime you think of the request in prayer, do not ask God again but instead, thank him for the answer. Thank him for loving you enough to hear and answer your prayer. The Bible says that God will inhabit your praise. As you praise him, you are being filled with God's Spirit and his presence. This only adds power to your prayer.

Billie, be specific when you talk to God. He loves you enough to answer your prayer. Believe in him. He does answer prayer today!

Dear Superniki Purple,
My son's young widow is thinking of re-marrying already. It has only been a year

since he died. This disgrace is breaking my heart. How can I stop her? Addie

Dear Addie,

Obviously you loved your son very much. If he were still alive, you would do everything possible to make him happy. Your son probably loved his wife very much and did everything possible to make her happy. She was important to him. If he really loved her, he would not want her to spend the rest of her young life unhappy and lonely. If she cannot be happy alone, then don't drive her from you by condemning her. This will be your loss. You must realize that she is a woman with a whole future ahead of her. Realize that she loved your son but that she has room in her heart to love another. This is no disgrace to you or your son.

Your son would like to think that his wife was enjoying a healthy, happy life. He wouldn't want her to marry the first man who comes along. However, if she chose your son, she has proven her good taste. Let her know that you are behind her and that you are praying for her that she will marry the right man. If she jumps into marriage because she is lonely and confused, she will be headed for problems. But if she knows that you are with her and are praying with her, and knows that God is the only Comforter, and that he loves her and her future, then she probably will not marry as an escape.

When she chooses to remarry, you must not be bitter. This is your son's wife. The fact that she wants to remarry is a great compliment to your son. If their marriage had been miserable, she might not have wanted to remarry for fear of another flop. If their marriage was wonderful, she would want to recapture at least a part of what she had with your son.

When she remarries, don't feel that you have been forsaken. If you are the kind of mother who raised such a fine son, your daughter-in-law will continue to love you.

Dear Superniki Purple,

I became a Christian because I didn't want to go to Hell. I was so scared that I decided to live right. But I find there is no joy in my life. What's wrong? Tony

Dear Tony,

Your comment reminds me of the girl who got married because she was afraid she would be an old maid. What sort of marriage could she expect? When you don't sin because you don't want to go to Hell, you are missing the most delightfully happy experience any human being can possibly have. There is great joy in being married for the right reasons and there is even greater joy in being a Christian for the right reason. And that reason, of course, is love.

Now even after a good marriage, the love can die and the marriage can be perfectly miserable. When you look into the reasons, too often you will find that the appreciation was gone, the expressions of love were forgotten, neglect took over.

The same can and does apply to Jesus. You can be enthused about what Jesus has done for you. You can be thrilled with his love and his goodness to you. But neglect him, forget to tell him how much you love him, forget to talk to him, forget to pray, forget to read your Bible, and soon your relationship will wither as the marriage relationship can do.

You can't love Jesus only when you see that he has done something extra special for you. A wife doesn't love her husband just when he buys her something. You don't appreciate Jesus just when you feel like it. You don't appreciate your wife just now and then. This must be a constant thing. When all negative, judging, criticizing thoughts leave — when your heart is filled with love for Jesus, you will find an excitement that I could never describe. You will become aware of his great love for you and he will make you into his *Superniki* — and nothing can be better than that!

Dear Superniki Purple,
I would like to really dedicate my life to God but I'm afraid that he will ask me to do something that I can't do or wouldn't want to do. I'm all mixed up; I want to do what's right and yet I'm afraid. Nita

Dear Nita,

The first thing you need to realize is that Jesus loves you. He will not ask you to do anything that you could not do. He will be with you to help you, and with him all things are possible. You do not have to fear God's will for your life. "God's will for your life is what you would choose for yourself if you knew all the facts."

One of my favorite Bible stories is the story of David. While I admire David greatly, I would hate to have to fight anyone with a little slingshot, much less fight a giant. Why, I couldn't even hit the side of a barn with a slingshot. But let's look at David's childhood. What did he do daily? What did he do well? What did he really enjoy doing? Shooting his slingshot, of course. He spent many happy hours shooting his slingshot. No one had to force David to shoot it. He did it because he really wanted to . . . and yet, that was the very thing that God used. He used the one thing that David enjoyed doing and could do well — that same slingshot killed the giant and won a great battle. The Lord did not ask him to do a strange and difficult task. No, he had him do something that he was familiar with and enjoyed doing — shooting his slingshot.

Nita, you do not have to be afraid to say, "Lord, take my life and use it anyway you will," because we know that God is a good God. God will not ask us to do something strange — something that we can't handle. He will use whatever you can do — no matter what.

Checking back in the Bible you will find that God used many strange things: David had the sling; Dorcas had a needle; Moses' rod was used often; Shamgar had an ox goad; and you remember Mary's ointment. God used all of these things and many more.

Dear Superniki Purple,

I work with a bunch of sinners and I feel out of place. I really like my job, though. Should I change jobs because of the people I work with? Liz

Dear Liz,

What a marvelous opportunity you have to be a shining light for Jesus! Jesus must love you very much to have placed you in such surroundings. The flame of one tiny match makes a brilliant light when placed in total darkness. Your light will be Jesus, of course, for he is the light of the world. The Scripture says, "Let everything you do be done in love," and of course love means God for "God is love." You cannot force your religion down the throats of people. They will not stand for embarrassment, ridicule, or any other form of unkindness. As you have a song in your heart, and kindness in all you do, you will become a shining example of God's love.

You should be like the little boy who walked around with a huge grin on his face, eating ice cream. The more he licked that ice cream the more everyone around him wanted what he had! Not only did they want it, but they made every effort to get some for themselves. Jesus is like ice cream. If you walk around enjoying being a Christian, living a victorious life, happy in Jesus, not complaining and being unkind, you will stand out from the world much more than that little match in the darkness.

Be glad if you work with many non-believers. Remember that you don't plant corn in the middle of a field of corn — you plant corn in an empty field so that it will grow. You have been planted in an empty field so that the harvest might be great. Rejoice, for Jesus loves you!

Dear Superniki Purple,

I have tried warning people that they are going to Hell if they don't change their ways, and all it gets me is trouble. No one will listen to me. What am I doing wrong? Murray

Dear Murray,

It's a shame that we Christians don't take a few lessons from the advertising world. It has been interesting to watch the TV battle of commercials for and against cigarettes. On one program you see beautiful people who are supposed to be happy and successful because they smoke and then on the next program you see the warning that cigarettes could kill you. After a few months of this, the sale of cigarettes was going up. The Cancer Society became very upset and so they discovered what we Christians fail to discover. The American public will not listen to warnings. And so the Cancer Society revamped their advertising and now the commercials are so outstanding that even non-smokers like us are fascinated with the commercials. The commercial I prefer shows how the father smokes and the darling young son imitates the father. Instead of trying to scare the non-scarable Americans into stopping for their own good, the Cancer Society tries to appeal to the smoker's sense of responsibility.

But still the cigarette sales grow higher. Why? It's so simple. When you see a TV commercial on cigarettes, you see the most successful, best-looking, happy people. Somehow the subconscious gets the crazy notion that *just maybe* smoking could fill the desire that is deep within that nothing else has filled and so the poor desperate public tries smoking, but they find that smoking isn't the answer. It wasn't all that it was cracked up to be. But by then they are hooked on the habit and so they smoke without obtaining the results that they had hoped for.

Now we have Jesus to sell, and unlike cigarettes, his results are always more than we expect instead of a letdown. The approach of scaring people with Hell has proven to be only slightly effective. People nowadays will turn you off when you try to scare them. But the commercial of the happy, successful people smoking — that attracts people. The best advertising you can do for Jesus is to be happy, enjoy life, live as Jesus would have you live, practice his principles and prove that the Scriptures really work. If your life demonstrates the love and power of God, you, too, will be a good advertisement. People are watching you and your reactions. You are the best Christian that somebody knows. The way you act and react will be your commercial for Jesus.

Dear Superniki Purple,

My neighbor lets her kids go dirty. It drives me mad! They have plenty of money and yet the kids look like beggars. I have given them clothes but she won't keep them clean. What can I do? Carolyn

Dear Carolyn,

You are suffering from the same "disease" that plagues many of us. The thing that is important to you — clean clothes — obviously is not important to your neighbor. We are all prone to push our values off on others. I, too, am guilty. I have cleaned house for someone only to return a few days later to see that my labor was in vain. I know people who have gone to great inconvenience to cook or sew or do something else for someone only to find it unappreciated. It seems unfair.

It took a big blow to wake me up to my own "pushy ways." We were having guests and I made my specialty — meatballs. They smelled delicious and I was looking forward to serving them.

While I was out of the room, my well-meaning guest added several ingredients that I do not like in meatballs. She is a better cook than I and her intentions were good. She thought she could improve on my cooking. I was furious!

Why, she just ruined my delicious meatballs and my meal! Her good intentions only gave me indigestion. But they did wake me up to my own actions.

It was important to her that certain ingredients be added. It's important to you that your children have clean play clothes. How ever, the same things may not be important to someone else.

If a clean kitchen is important to me, then I should keep my kitchen clean and let yours be a mess if it isn't important to you. If it's important to you that you get your hair done weekly, then do it but don't look down your pretty nose at me if mine is a disheveled mess.

Instead of feeling responsible for the dirty clothes of the neighbors, keep *your* children clean and let the neighbor do whatever is important to her. We are all strong individualists and should not try to remake others to fit our patterns.

Just be sweet and loving and don't place great emphasis on unimportant things. The only really important thing is the peace and love of God. As you love your neighbors and don't feel guilty about your own children, you will all be happier.

Dear Superniki Purple,

I have the worst luck with neighbors. Everywhere I move, I get lousy neighbors. Do you have any suggestions? Kay

Dear Kay,

Neighbors are just people. Most people are mirrors. They react to you. There's an old story that I love. There was a wagon-load of people who entered a small town and stopped the first man that they saw. They asked the old man what kind of people lived in the town. They were considering settling there. The old man thought for a moment and then asked them what kind of neighbors they had had in the town that they had just left. After a few minutes, they replied that they had had the worst luck. Their neighbors had been gossipy, selfish, thoughtless people who complained constantly. The old man shook his head sadly and replied that they would have exactly the same kind of neighbors in this town. And so the wagon-load of people drove on.

Presently a second wagon-load arrived in the same town and stopped the same old man and asked the same question about the kind of neighbors they would have if they settled there. The old man asked them the same question. The people were quick to answer with nothing but praise for the neighbors they had just left. They couldn't say enough nice things about them. The old man smiled and said that they would find exactly the same kind of neighbors in this town.

People will react to whatever we are. If we are kind, people will react with kindness. If we are hateful, people will be unkind to us. Try going into any store and be extra polite to the tired clerk and see if she isn't polite to you. Just see if you don't rate a smile even though she's bushed. By the same token, be rude and see if you don't get a little rudeness in return. "Do unto others as you would have them do unto you," is certainly not outdated. It is to our advantage to try it.

Kay, if you want good neighbors, you be a good neighbor first. To have a friend, you must first be a friend.

Dear Superniki Purple,

I'm a successful woman. I have an exceptionally good job, I'm involved in a dozen different clubs, I teach a Sunday school class, and I have many friends who think I'm just about it. The only person who is not impressed with me is my husband and he's the only one who counts. What have I done wrong? Margie

Dear Margie,

You sound like quite a woman! Perfect might be a good name for you — or is it "too perfect"? All too often women try so hard to prove themselves that they actually succeed. They show the world that they can amount to something special. They become the greatest hostess, get in the center of every activity that comes along, make friends easily and have self-confidence in all they do. There are many who have succeeded in making their husbands miserable.

The flaw lies in the fact that your husband is human and wants a "human" wife. When you become so great, you climb out of the human category and into the "too perfect" category. Your husband will have a difficult time keeping up with you and all too often will begin to feel inferior to you. The more people brag about your accomplishments, the less he will like himself. The more you show him up — even if unintentionally — the less he will like you.

This trait isn't limited to husbands — we are all subject to it to some degree. How well I remember when my mother came down off her pedestal and became my dearest friend. I discovered that she was human; she wasn't really perfect. Instead of driving me away, it made me love her all the more and want to be her friend. For years there was one girl whom I avoided. I felt so inferior to her that I was uncomfortable when she was around. She had

succeeded at everything — she was brilliant,
beautiful, successful, and married a wealthy
man. She knew all the right things to do and
say. I avoided her because I liked myself less
when she was around. Then one day I discovered that she was human — she had problems, too. I was so amazed that I could help
her that I immediately began to love her and
we became good friends. When the feelings of
inferiority left, we were able to become
friends.

Margie, don't try to outdo your husband.
Instead of trying to outdo your friends and
build yourself up, build up your husband and
at the same time establish a solid marriage. A
wise wife never makes her husband look inferior.

That doesn't mean that you have to stop
learning or stop being proper. The perfect example is that when you walk with a two-year-
old, you walk at his pace. If you try to drag
him at your normal pace, the child will soon
get tired out and start crying and you will end
up carrying him or being annoyed — or both.
If you will slow your pace to fit his short legs,
you will both enjoy the walk. Slowing down
doesn't make you as weak as the child but
makes your life and the walk more pleasant.
Slowing down to your husband's pace doesn't
mean stop doing all the right things but it does

mean that you will enjoy your life together. Soon he will catch up and surpass you even as a child soon is able to out-walk an adult. The Bible says that the man is to be the head of the house — the stronger. Let him be and you will find that he, too, will think that you are Mrs. Wonderful.

The secret of conquering inferiority, of course, is in knowing that you are a child of the king. You are God's. When you discover that God loves you and you are important to him, inferiority complexes will have no place in your life. Until your husband discovers his own importance, you will have to help him by not showing off or rubbing it in that you are more successful. When you make him happy, you will be happier. Marriage works that way.

Dear Superniki Purple,

It annoys me the way good, decent people are mistreated. Why is it that bad things always happen to the nicest people? What happened to the Scripture that says "All things work together for good"? Evelyn

Dear Evelyn,

The Scripture is still very true. The Bible says "All things work *together* for good to them that love God." The point you are missing is the "together."

I make a delicious lemon cake. I use five eggs, two cups of sugar, two cups of flour, two sticks of butter and two teaspoons of lemon flavoring. If you tried to eat any of those ingredients all by itself, you would find it distasteful if not downright sickening. The very thought of raw eggs makes me nauseated. Trying to eat dry tasteless flour would be repulsive. And while I like butter with something, I'd hate to have to eat two sticks of it alone. That delicious cake is made up of some unappealing ingredients. And yet when they are all mixed together, they create a very tasty cake.

The same applies to life. We all have wondered why God allowed such terrible things to happen to nice people. But the Bible says that his ways are far above our ways and we cannot understand them but we can trust him.

Occasionally he allows us to see the reason so that our faith will be strengthened for the times when we will not see the reason.

A friend of mine was in a real financial bind. There was quite a strain in meeting the bills. One day there was a fire in their garage. They were terrified that their house might burn, too. The firemen traipsed in and out of the house until their carpet appeared to be ruined. While they were grateful that their house didn't burn, they did lose quite a few things in the garage. The insurance man estimated the damage and presented them with a check. The check was enough to pay for repairing the garage with enough left over to get them out of their financial bind. The husband repaired the burnt washing machine and cleaned the carpet. The other things which were lost were of no sentimental value and were only being stored there since they were no longer necessary. The moments of agony while the fire raged, the inconvenience of repairing the garage, and the time and trouble spent in repairing the washing machine and cleaning the carpet was nothing to compare with the relief of paying off the bills.

Another friend quit his job during an angry dispute. I felt so sorry about his being without a job. However, a few weeks passed and I heard that he had a real good job "back home." His family had wanted to go back home for years but he just couldn't bring himself to quit such a good job without having another waiting for him. The bad thing — the dispute — turned out to be very good because it pushed him into doing what he really wanted to do anyway.

One of my girl friends was jilted at the altar. She was very much in love and took the rejection extremely hard. With time she got over it and met and married a delightful man. Her marriage turned out to be exceptionally happy. The man who jilted her continued to be a heel. Comparing the two men years later, it's a cinch that she is better off for having been jilted.

Unfortunately, we don't always know the reasons behind all the things that happen to us and other "good people." But there is always a reason, and the "bad" will always work together for our good. When we love Jesus and ask him to control our lives, nothing, absolutely nothing, can happen to us nor involve us unless he allows it. Surely he will keep his promise that "all things work together for good."

If you will remember the "together," you will not be unhappy with the way God runs things. You can trust him with your life. When disaster hits your life, expect God to make something wonderful out of it and he will. The disaster may be just a stepping-stone into something very exciting. Remember, Jesus loves you!

Dear Superniki Purple,

I have been reading in national magazines where the young people are finding way-out religions that have adventure and participation. I think they have a good point. There's no fun in the religion of the older generation. If I weren't so old, I'd join them in their search for reality. Monk

Dear Monk,

Instead of joining them in some odd religion, why don't you join the people today (yes, even in the older generation's religion) who are finding a thrill out of knowing God. I spoke with a Baptist minister in the first weeks of 1970. This is what had just happened to him.

He was in a distant city when the Lord told him to go to Houston on a certain day. Yes, Monk, the Lord will speak to those who have learned to listen to his voice, always checking carefully with the Bible to make certain that everything they "hear" is in agreement with the Bible. Anyway, the minister closed his meeting and went to the airport. There was only one flight out for Houston and it was booked solid. There wasn't a chance of getting aboard. But the Lord had told him to go on that day and the Lord knew all about the planes. So he went to the ticket counter and asked for a ticket. The young lady told him that it would be foolish for him to buy a ticket because there had been no cancellations and he would just have to get a refund. He told the lady that the Lord had told him to get on that plane. So he checked his luggage and bought a ticket against her better judgment.

Time passed and no cancellations came through. The plane arrived, loaded, and was preparing to take off when suddenly over the intercom in the large airport came the following message: "Reverend Hank Dreher. You were right. God has a seat for you. Report to . . ." He rushed aboard. The hostess came over to him and told him that she had majored in math in college and had made A's and had been a hostess for several years, but she had never miscounted the seats before. He told her about God reserving the seat for him. Then he went on to tell her about the love and excitement of knowing God.

Monk, if you experienced something like that — and this man does daily — you wouldn't be seeking an "odd" religion. You would want to experience Jesus Christ who is the only reality and the best thing that ever happened!

Dear Superniki Purple,

Many of my friends come to me for advice. I tell them about the Lord and that he is the answer. It doesn't seem to soak in at all. They look so blank and unconcerned. I feel like they come back out of habit instead of being interested. How do you get through to people? Sandie

Dear Sandie,

The fact that your friends keep coming back is a good indication that they are getting at

least some of what you are telling them. You
can't judge the results of what you are saying.
There is no way for you to know what is going on inside of the person you are talking to
about the Lord.

Many years ago a friend of mine invited
her friend to attend church to hear a special
speaker. All during the service the friend sat
there looking bored to pieces while she peeled
off her nail polish. My friend was just furious.
She had gone to considerable trouble to get
her there and she seemed totally bored. After
service, my friend really blasted her for her
unconcern. She looked dumbfounded and pro-
ceeded to repeat the sermon almost *verbatim*.
Not only had she been listening, she absorbed
what she heard. My friend had been so busy
judging her that she hadn't heard any of the
sermon.

Once my mother was giving an object lesson on ceramics to two Baptist ministers who
were visiting my sick grandmother. One minister looked bored to pieces. Mother was a little
embarrassed that she had started the object
lesson. She finished as quickly as possible and
they left without any comment. She felt as if
she had just wasted their valuable time. However, the following day the minister's wife
called and asked Mother to give the object lesson in church on the following Sunday night

because her husband had just raved over it and said everyone should hear it.

Sandie, there is no way for you to tell the results you are getting. You cannot judge others. The results of whatever you say are up to God. You can trust him to get through to your friends. He knows what he is doing through you. Do not be discouraged; remember that you are not to judge anyone or anything. Just love God and others.

Dear Reader,

I hope you have enjoyed this book. But more important, I hope you enjoy Jesus Christ in your life daily. If you have not given him a chance to show you the excitement of his love, what are you waiting for? You will never be sorry if you will allow Jesus to come into your heart and make you into his Superniki! Life is wonderful! Life is to be enjoyed! This isn't an endurance contest — this is life we are talking about! If you aren't completely happy with yourself right now, why not give Jesus a chance to prove to you that you can be happy and you can be Superniki! Let Second Corinthians 2:14 become your motto: "Now thanks be unto God, which *always* causeth us to triumph in Christ."

There is an answer for all problems. That answer is Jesus! If you do not know him personally, I invite you to discover the *best thing* that could ever happen to you. I'd like to introduce you to my *friend, Jesus.* He will make your life worth living. He will put a song in your heart and a sparkle in your eyes.

Always remember — Jesus loves *you;* and so does . . .

Superniki Purple